ANDY MURRAY

A **LiFe** STORY

Stephen Davies

Illustrated by **Sarah Papworth**

■SCHOLASTIC

For my mother-in-law Pammi –
Scottish tennis player and Andy Murray superfan

Published in the UK by Scholastic, 2022
Euston House, 24 Eversholt Street, London, NW1 1DB
Scholastic Ireland, 89E Lagan Road, Dublin Industrial Estate, Glasnevin,
Dublin, D11 HP5F

SCHOLASTIC and associated logos are trademarks and/or
registered trademarks of Scholastic Inc.

Text © Stephen Davies, 2022
Illustrations by Sarah Papworth © Scholastic, 2022

ISBN 978 07023 1682 1

A CIP catalogue record for this book is available from the British Library.

Printed by CPI Group (UK) Ltd, Croydon, CR0 4YY
Paper made from wood grown in sustainable forests and other
controlled sources.

1 3 5 7 9 10 8 6 4 2

www.scholastic.co.uk

CONTENTS

INTRODUCTION

Prince William stood on the stage in front of 15,000 people. It was December 2016 and he had come to the Genting Arena in Birmingham to take part in a very special ceremony, the BBC Sports Personality of the Year Awards. The main award at this event is given to the British sportsperson voted most outstanding of the year.

The prince was sharing the spotlight with a world-famous athlete called Jessica Ennis-Hill. As the crucial moment arrived, he handed her a black envelope containing the name of the winner, chosen by the British public from a list of sixteen sportspeople.

Who would it be? Footballer Jamie Vardy, whose goals had helped Leicester City to win the Premier League at odds of 5,000–1? Nicola Adams, who had successfully defended her Olympic boxing title? Or perhaps Nick Skelton, who had won a showjumping gold medal at the age of fifty-eight – sixteen years after falling from a horse and breaking his neck.

Jessica Ennis-Hill opened the envelope. She raised her microphone and a dazzling smile spread across her face. 'The BBC Sports Personality of the Year is...'

World-class athletes shuffled in their seats. Fifteen thousand people in the arena and five million at home all held their breath.

'Andy Murray!'

Lights flashed. Music blared. A slim, nervous-looking young man appeared on a massive screen behind the stage and was handed a silver trophy.

Awards host Gary Lineker grinned from ear to ear. 'Congratulations, Andy Murray!' he proclaimed. 'You are the first person to win that trophy on three separate occasions!'

It was true. Five sportsmen including Andy had won the award twice, but no one had ever won it three times. It was a staggering achievement.

What had Andy done to achieve these honours? How did a young boy from a small town in Scotland grow up to become one of the most celebrated

British sportspeople that have ever lived?

Read on to find out!

TENNIS

Tennis is a popular sport where players use rackets to hit a fuzzy ball back and forth over a net. Each time your opponent fails to hit the ball back, you score a point.

- Four points win you a game.
- Six games win you a set.
- Two sets (or three in some tournaments win you the match.

Tennis is sometimes played on grass and sometimes on clay or another hard surface. You can play singles (with one player on one side of the net and one player on the other side) or doubles (two players on each side of the net).

Tennis players are some of the fittest sportspeople in the world, using speed, strength and skill to win points. To win a whole match, they also need stamina – the ability to play well not just for a few minutes but for hours, if necessary.

ENERGY

On 15 May 1987, Russia launched a huge rocket called *Energiya* (Energy) into space. As it rose into the air, a baby was being born in Glasgow, Scotland – a baby who would have plenty of energy himself, and would also end up among the stars.

Andy grew up in the Scottish town of Dunblane, an hour's drive from the capital city, Edinburgh. Dunblane is named after a gentle monk called Blane who (according to one local legend) was able to make fire with little thunderbolts from his fingers!

Andy lived with his mum, Judy, his dad, William, and his big brother, Jamie. His

Energiya rocket

mum was a tennis coach, working with young people to help them improve their tennis. She loved tennis with all her heart and wanted her own sons to enjoy it, too. When Andy was two years old, she put a tennis racket in his hand and threw a sponge ball for him to hit. Andy swung and missed. She threw him another. He missed that, too. Over the following weeks and months, little Andy missed thousands more balls. His brother Jamie had good coordination and learned to hit the ball from a very early age, but Andy showed no sign of tennis skill whatsoever.

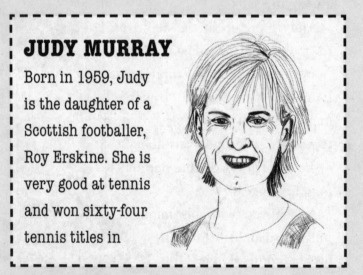

JUDY MURRAY

Born in 1959, Judy is the daughter of a Scottish footballer, Roy Erskine. She is very good at tennis and won sixty-four tennis titles in

Scotland, including the Scottish Grass Court Championship. She was known for being fast around the court and extremely determined, chasing every single ball that came on to her side of the court. When she was not playing tennis, she did various different jobs, including being a travelling salesperson for a firm that made sweets and chocolates. Eventually she became a full-time tennis coach.

"BACK YOURSELF. INVEST IN YOURSELF. BELIEVE IN YOURSELF."

Judy Murray, Twitter (August 2020)

Andy's early failures at hitting a ball did not put him off. He and Jamie played tennis whenever and wherever they could. They played tennis on the kitchen table, using cereal boxes as a net. They played 'Swingball' in the garden, hitting a ball on a string back and forth between them.

They even played in their gran's living room, but only after she had carefully removed any breakable ornaments.

All of this tennis was having an effect. Andy's coordination was getting better. Now he could hit the ball more often than not. At age five he started to play on a proper tennis court, at the tennis club close to his house. He was not very good, but he had a competitive spirit and he persevered. Not long after starting to play at the club, he announced to his mum:

"I WANT TO PLAY A PROPER MATCH!"

FOREHAND AND BACKHAND

These are the two basic strokes used in all racket games, including tennis, squash, racketball and badminton:

Forehand
If you are right-handed and the ball comes

towards you on your right side, you should play a forehand. Keep your eye on the ball and hit it with the middle of your racket.

Backhand

If you are right-handed and the ball comes towards you on your left side, you should play a backhand. Andy Murray plays his backhand with both hands on the racket, for extra power.

If you are left-handed, you play forehands on your left side and backhands on your right.

As well as playing tennis, Andy loved collecting football stickers and watching cartoons on TV. His favourite cartoon was *Teenage Mutant Hero Turtles*, a programme about a gang of talking turtles solving crimes and defeating bad guys. Andy loved other sports, too. He played a lot of football and at home he enjoyed wrestling matches with Jamie.

Apart from his brother, Andy's best pal was his hamster, Whisky. He spent hours playing with him, and even built a climbing frame for him to get from the floor to the sink. You can guess what happened after that – Whisky escaped down the plughole and was never seen again!

Andy's grandparents (Judy's mum and dad) lived in Dunblane, too, and they often collected Andy and Jamie from school. Sometimes they took the boys to the local tennis club and sometimes to the toyshop that they owned.

Young Andy

Pink shorts

Andy enjoyed watching tennis on TV and his favourite player was Andre Agassi. As well as being a superb tennis player, Andre had a unique fashion sense, wearing brightly coloured shirts, shorts and headbands to keep his long hair away from his face. For three years, Andre refused invitations to play at the Wimbledon tennis tournament in London, because players there have to wear all-white tennis clothes.

ANDRE AGASSI

Born: 29 April 1970, Las Vegas, USA

Nationality: American

Height: 180 cm

Weight: 80 kg

Plays: right-handed

Highest world ranking: 1

Number of major tournaments won: 8

When Andre was young, his father made him practise for hours against 'the dragon', a machine that fired tennis balls at Andre for him to hit back. His shots became more and more powerful, and at the age of eighteen Andre was already ranked number one in the world. His style of play was to stand at the back of the court (called the baseline) and hit the ball left, right, left, right. His opponents got tired from all that running, and Andre gained the nickname 'The Punisher'.

In 1994, when Andre Agassi played in the final of the US Open, the most important tennis tournament in America, seven-year-old Andy Murray watched the match on TV wearing one of Andre's signature outfits: blue denim shorts over bright pink cycling shorts. To complete the costume, Andy wore a long, blond ponytail clipped on to the back of his cap!

Andre Agassi's dad had put a lot of pressure on

him to practise and succeed, but Andy Murray's mum was very different. She encouraged and supported her sons, but she never forced them to play tennis. All she wanted was for them to enjoy the game. Andy practised against humans, not against a dragon-like tennis machine, and whenever he wanted to take a break from tennis, his mum let him.

The Saltire Minibus

As they improved, Andy, Jamie and their tennis-playing friends started travelling to tournaments in other towns. Judy Murray drove them to tournaments in England in a minibus decorated with Scottish flags.

The Scottish flag is a white cross on a blue background. It is sometimes called the 'St Andrew's Cross' or the 'Saltire'.

Scottish flag

Playing in tournaments helped Jamie and Andy to improve their tennis skills. But of course, Jamie was always that little bit older and stronger than Andy, and always beat him in matches.

TENNIS TOURNAMENTS

Most tennis tournaments are 'knockout' competitions. If you lose your first match, you are unfortunately out of the tournament. If you win your first match, you go through to the second round, where you play one of the other winners. And so it goes on. Winners go through and losers get 'knocked out'. At the 'quarter-final' stage, just eight players are left. The quarter-final winners go through to the semi-finals, and the semi-final winners go through to the final. Whoever wins the final is crowned the winner of the whole tournament.

tennis racket

When Andy was ten, he and Jamie played at a tournament in Solihull, near Birmingham, UK and they both managed to get through to the final. Then something amazing happened. For the first time ever, Andy beat his older brother in a proper match. To everyone's amazement, Andy won the trophy.

This was a huge turning point for young Andy. He had beaten his brilliant older brother, and now anything seemed possible. On the way back in the minibus, Andy was in a joyful mood, crowing non-stop about his victory. Jamie lost his temper and thumped his little brother on the hand, hurting one of Andy's fingers quite badly. Even as an adult, Andy's fingernail is still wonky – a reminder of his first ever victory against his brother.

Sadly, there were arguments at home, too. Andy's mum and dad were not getting on well with each other, and they decided to separate. Judy Murray moved out of the house, while Andy and Jamie continued to live there with their dad, William.

WILLIAM MURRAY

Andy Murray's dad is a hard-working businessman, who owns several shops selling snacks and newspapers. As a father, William was quite strict. Whenever Andy forgot to do his homework or got into trouble at school, his dad was very cross with him. In his free time, William played squash, golf or five-a-side football, and was extremely competitive at all of these sports. With such sporty parents, it is no wonder that Andy and Jamie grew up loving sports.

Judy stayed in Dunblane and saw her sons almost every day, mostly on the tennis court. She knew that modern tennis players need special 'weapons' – powerful, point-winning shots that can beat the toughest opponents. Not only did she teach Andy and Jamie these shots, she also taught them a deep understanding of tennis tactics, so that they could select which kind of shot to play at each moment in a game.

Forget the Football

As well as playing tennis, Andy played a lot of football. He was so good, he was even invited to do some training with Rangers football club in Scotland.

In the end, though, tennis was where Andy's heart lay. One day, his dad came to the tennis club to collect him for football training. "Forget the football," Andy told him. "I'm sticking with my tennis training."

Andy's mum knew that he had the potential to become a very special tennis player, and also that she was no longer the best person to train him. When Andy was eleven years old, she asked a young Scottish player called Leon Smith whether he would be willing to work with Andy. Leon was twenty-two at the time. He was funny and cool, and young Andy liked him a lot. The two of them became practice partners. Before long, they would be travelling all over the world together in search of tennis glory.

THE YOUNG WARRIOR

Andy Murray's middle name is Barron, which means 'young warrior'. It was an appropriate name for a young tennis player who seemed to get stronger and more skilful with every tournament he played in.

In December 1999, Leon took Andy to play in a big tournament in Miami, USA. Known as the Orange Bowl, it attracted the best young tennis players in the world. There were two competitions for boys, one for ages twelve and under, and one for ages fourteen and under. Twelve-year-old Andy won match after match in the twelve-and-under competition, and got all the way through to the final.

In the final, Andy showed the special understanding of tennis tactics that his mum had taught him. The spectators were amazed by the variety of special shots that Andy used, including volleys, lobs, smashes and drop shots.

FOUR CUNNING TENNIS SHOTS

Each of these shots can be played either forehand or backhand.

Volley

A volley is when you hit the ball before it bounces, giving your opponent less time to react. The best time to do this is when you are standing near the net.

Lob

A lob is when you hit the ball so high over your opponent's head that they cannot reach it, even by jumping. The best time to try this shot is when your opponent is standing near the net.

Smash

A smash is when you reach up over your head and whack the ball down into your opponent's court. It is a such a powerful shot, it is usually impossible for your opponent to return it.

Drop shot
A drop shot is when you hit the ball so softly that it only just goes over the net, then bounces twice before your opponent can reach it. Andy loves this shot!

Andy played beautiful, flowing tennis. He won the final and was presented with the trophy, a gleaming silver fruit bowl. Of course, his coach Leon was absolutely thrilled. On the plane home, Leon kept thinking to himself, 'This boy is one of the world's best talents.'

When Andy got home, he gave the Orange Bowl trophy to his gran and suggested that she could make a big fruit salad in it. She did exactly that, and the whole family ate the fruit salad with ice cream on Christmas Day!

In 2001, at the age of fourteen, Andy entered

Les Petits As, one of the most prestigious junior tournaments in Europe, held in the French town of Tarbes. In the semi-final, he played a skinny teenager called Novak Djokovic, who was exactly one week younger than Andy. Neither of them knew it at the time, but Novak would become one of Andy's biggest tennis rivals. That day in France, Andy managed to beat Novak. "You kicked my butt pretty bad!" Novak told him years later.

As well as being born within seven days of each other, Andy Murray and Novak Djokovic had something else in common. They were both keen Monopoly players. Andy played at home in Dunblane. He was super-competitive and used to tip the board on to the floor if he was losing. Novak played in a basement in Belgrade in Serbia, whilst sheltering from air raids. His country was at war, and bombs were dropping from planes all over the city.

A Close Call

Andy was through to the final of Les Petis As, the last match of the tournament, where his opponent was a lively Russian boy called Alexandre Krasnoroutskiy. There were more than 2,000 people in the crowd, eager to see who would be the winner and who would be the runner-up.

Andy played the same clever, flowing tennis he had played against Novak in the semi-final, and he managed to reach match point. Match point is exactly what it sounds like – you need just one more point to win the match. If you win that point, you win the match. If your opponent wins the point, they have 'saved' match point, and the game continues.

On match point, the two boys bashed the ball back and forth across the net, both of them desperate to win the point. Suddenly, Andy saw an opportunity to play a drop shot. He took a big swing, pretending that he was going to hit the ball hard, but then at the very last second he slowed his racket and dinked the ball gently over the net.

Alexandre charged forward, knowing that if he let the ball bounce twice on his side of the court, he would lose the match – and the tournament. Andy sprinted forward, too. If the drop shot did not win the point instantly, his next volley would. Two thousand people held their breath. The Russian teenager managed to reach the drop shot just in time. With a flick of his racket, he scooped the ball up off the court before it could bounce twice. Andy watched in horror as the ball cleared the net on his left. He launched himself towards it, but could not quite reach it. The ball sailed past Andy's racket and landed in the court behind him. Alexandre had saved match point.

Tennis matches can go on for hours, but when two brilliant players meet each other, the match is often decided by tiny moments in a game – a single point here or there. After Alexandre Krasnoroutskiy saved that crucial point, things started to go his way. The Russian ended up winning the match – and the tournament. Andy was gutted to be the runner-up. He phoned his mum in tears and told her just how close he had come to winning the trophy.

In the Firing Line

Even though Andy had not won at Tarbes, he had played amazingly. Tennis reporters across the country were beginning to believe that the young Scottish tennis player could become one of the greats. A BBC camera crew went to Dunblane and Andy appeared on the BBC news, showing off his powerful serve.

The serve is how each point in tennis begins – you toss the ball high into the air and swing your racket hard to smack the ball over the net into your opponent's court. Racket in hand, the BBC reporter scrambled after Andy's bullet-like serves, but could not return a single one. "This is what I call being in the firing line," the reporter gasped. "Serves of up to 115 miles per hour, and that's from a fourteen-year-old schoolboy!"

When asked about his ambitions, Andy's reply was very specific. "Hopefully I'll be playing at senior Wimbledon in four years, and at junior Wimbledon in two years."

THE FOUR MAJORS

The four most important tennis tournaments in the world are called the four 'majors'.

The oldest and most prestigious of the four is Wimbledon. It takes place every year in London, and all of the world's biggest tennis stars go there, hoping to do well.

Australian Open: January (hard court)

French Open: May–June (clay court)

Wimbledon: June–July (grass court)

US Open: August–September (hard court)

The four major tournaments are sometimes called the 'Grand Slam' tournaments. If a player wins each major at least once in their lifetime, that is called a 'Career Grand Slam'. If a player wins all four majors in one year, that is called a 'Calendar Grand Slam'. Only five players have ever achieved a Calendar

Grand Slam: Don Budge (1938), Maureen
Connolly Brinker (1953), Rod Laver (twice –
in 1962 and 1969), Margaret Court (1970)
and Steffi Graf (1988).

Junior Wimbledon in two years and senior
Wimbledon in four. Could it happen? Andy and
those who knew him best were convinced that
the answer was yes.

GROWING UP

Andy was growing up fast. He spent less time watching *Teenage Mutant Hero Turtles* and more time watching James Bond films. Lots of actors have played super-spy James Bond, but Andy's favourite was a Scottish actor called Sean Connery. A shop in Dunblane did a two-for-one offer on Bond films, and Andy spent most of his pocket money on them.

Andy attended school every day from Monday to Friday, which did not leave much time for practising tennis. His international rivals, players like Novak Djokovic and Rafael Nadal, were playing tennis for four or five hours a day, but Andy was lucky if he played that much in a week. Moreover, Scotland is one of the wettest countries in the world. Have you ever tried playing tennis in the pouring rain? It is a nightmare. The ball absorbs water and loses its bounciness. The court becomes slippery, increasing your risk of falling over and hurting yourself.

What Andy needed was a special tennis school, a place where he could focus on tennis all day every day. Preferably in a sunny country, where he did not have to worry about waterlogged tennis balls and puddles on the court.

He went with his mum to visit the Sánchez -Casal Academy, a special tennis school in Barcelona, a city on the coast of Spain. The school was founded by two great Spanish tennis players, Emilio Sánchez and Sergio Casal. Emilio Sánchez met Andy and his mum, and showed them around the school. It had twenty-nine tennis courts, and the young people practising there seemed serious about becoming tennis stars. After the tour, fifteen-year-old Andy played thirty-seven-year-old Emilio at tennis – and won!

A Spanish Adventure

It was very expensive to attend the Sánchez -Casal Academy but Andy and his family managed to raise the money they needed. In September

2002, Andy boarded a plane and flew to Spain all on his own. Not many boys leave their family at the age of fifteen and move to another country. Andy had to be brave and independent. But he quickly began to love his new life in Spain. He lived with other boys in a dormitory above the classrooms. They played tennis for three hours every morning and for an hour and a half every afternoon. School lessons had to be fitted in at lunchtime and in the evenings.

Andy and his friends were very mischievous. They copied each other's homework. They played pranks on each other. They stayed up until after midnight and had to scurry back to their beds when they heard the dormitory mistress coming to check on them. Andy had a lot of fun and made some lifelong friends.

In 2003, some of the best players from the academy went on tour to South America. They played in tournaments in Colombia, Ecuador, Peru, Bolivia and Paraguay. Andy won the tournament in Colombia and did well in the others, too.

ACADEMY IN SPAIN

What did Andy learn at tennis school?

Technical: Andy already knew the different tennis shots, but these lessons taught him how to adjust the height, length, speed and power of each shot.

Tactical: he learned how to develop his playing style, how to understand his strengths and weaknesses, and how to form a different game plan for beating each opponent.

Physical: he worked out in the gym and learned what kinds of food he should eat to keep his body healthy.

Mental: Andy learned how to stay positive, how to cope with pressure and how to set himself realistic goals.

A Painful Setback

After the South America tour, Andy's knee started to hurt. Over the following weeks, it got worse and worse, until he could hardly walk. He had to leave his beloved tennis school and go back to Scotland.

Back home, Andy saw several different doctors, and eventually one of them worked out what was wrong. Andy had been born with a split kneecap. The knobbly bone on his knee was in two pieces, rather than one. Andy had to rest his knee until he was well enough to play again. He knew this problem could not be cured, so he would just have to learn to live with it, and not push it too hard.

One Man and his Dog

When Andy got back to playing tennis, he entered junior tournaments all over the world. That may sound glamorous, but it certainly was not. Junior tournaments rarely attract a big crowd, and Andy joked that he often found himself playing matches in front of "one man and his dog". The courts were not always in good condition. The changing rooms smelled of wee. Cockroaches scuttled underfoot. The toilet cubicles never seemed to have any toilet paper and, as for the showers, Andy shuddered even to think of them: bare pipes protruding from the wall, spewing cold, smelly water.

Conditions at the majors were better, though. In 2004, at the age of seventeen, Andy entered the junior US Open, which attracted plenty of spectators and not a single cockroach. Andy stayed in a posh hotel and played on beautiful tennis courts under bright lights. He played well all week and got through to the final.

Game Plan

In the final of the junior US Open, Andy played against Sergiy Stakhovsky, a brilliant young player from Ukraine. Andy was well prepared. He had watched a video of Sergiy's semi-final match and he knew that Sergiy liked to serve and volley. 'Serve and volley' is a tennis strategy where you run forward after serving. If your opponent manages to return your serve, you will be right there at the net to volley home a winner.

Andy worked out that he could beat Sergiy by returning the serve as low as possible. If he aimed for Sergiy's feet, the Ukrainian would have to volley up, not down. The ball would go up into the air, giving Andy a good chance of winning the point.

SERVING AND RETURNING

In a tennis match, players take turns to 'serve' and 'return'. You serve one game and your opponent returns. Your opponent serves the next game and you return.

Your serve needs to bounce inside the 'service box' on your opponent's side of the net, and you have two chances to make this happen. If your first serve goes into the net or bounces outside the service box, you get a second serve. But if you fluff your second serve, it is a called a '**double fault**' and your opponent gets a free point.

Serving gives you a slight advantage, so top players usually win their '**service games**'. Winning your own service games is not enough, though. To win a whole match, you will have to win at least one of your opponent's service games. This is called '**breaking serve**'.

Andy's plan worked. He served well in his own service games and he attacked his opponent's service games by returning the ball hard and low. In the third game of the match, Andy broke Sergiy's serve, and went on to win the set 6–4 (six games to four). In the second set, Andy broke Sergiy's serve not once but twice, winning the set 6–2.

When Andy won match point, the crowd jumped to their feet, applauding and cheering. He had won a junior Grand Slam tournament! He was thrilled and his family were very proud. Andy had to do lots of interviews the next morning, and when he arrived back at Edinburgh airport, there was a big group of photographers and reporters waiting for him. This was a small taste of fame, but it was nothing compared to what was coming next.

TURNING PRO

Andy Murray had a fantastic year in 2005. It began with Andy being called up to play in the Davis Cup, a prestigious tournament where nations compete against each other in teams. Andy was the youngest British player ever to play in the Davis Cup, a boy competing against grown men. He played in a fierce doubles match against Israel, and won.

It was around this time that Andy became a professional tennis player (sometimes called 'turning pro'). This meant that tennis was now his full-time job, his main way of earning money. As well as turning pro, he also turned eighteen. Most people remember their eighteenth birthday as a huge moment in their lives. In the UK, it is the day you officially become an adult. You are now allowed to vote, open a bank account and do all sorts of other grown-up things.

Many people have a big party to celebrate

turning eighteen, but not Andy. His life was all about tennis now, travelling from tournament to tournament. He spent the evening of his eighteenth birthday all alone in a hotel room in Germany. A young tennis player has to make sacrifices in order to achieve great things, and this was just another of those sacrifices.

Professional tennis players take part in tennis tournaments throughout the year, all over the world. The players criss-cross the globe in search of glory and cash prizes, and in an average year they fly over 100,000 miles. A typical February on the men's tour includes tournaments in the Netherlands, Qatar and Mexico, while the same month on the women's tour takes players to Russia, Dubai and France. The teenage Andy Murray was certainly no stranger to early morning alarm calls, airports and aeroplane food!

First Wimbledon

You remember that out-of-breath BBC reporter who asked Andy about his ambitions? Do you remember Andy's reply?

"HOPEFULLY I'LL BE PLAYING AT SENIOR WIMBLEDON IN FOUR YEARS, AND AT JUNIOR WIMBLEDON IN TWO YEARS."

Andy Murray, BBC interview (2001)

Exactly four years after that interview, Andrew 'Young Warrior' Murray walked out on to Court Two to play his first ever match at a senior Wimbledon tennis tournament. Andy was ranked 317th, which in theory meant that he was the 317th best player in the world. This was the second-lowest ranking of all the men in Wimbledon that year. But that did not matter to Andy. This was the most prestigious tournament in the world, and he was determined to enjoy every moment.

Andy's opponent in round one was George Bastl of Switzerland. George was thirty years old and he was ranked 146th in the world, much higher than Andy. It is always exciting when a low-ranked player beats a higher-ranked player, and that is exactly what happened on Court Two that day. Andy broke George's serve five times. His lobs and smashes made the TV commentator chuckle with pleasure, and he ended up winning the match 6–4, 6–2, 6–2.

After the match, Andy hung around and signed autographs for everyone who wanted one. He remembered how disappointed he had been at the age of seven when he queued for Andre Agassi's autograph and did not manage to get it. He did not want anyone else to feel that disappointment.

George Bastl was out of the tournament, and Andy Murray was through to the second round. His next opponent was Radek Štěpánek from the Czech (pronounced 'check') Republic. Radek's ranking was thirteenth in the world, more than 300 places higher than Andy!

Andy felt nervous walking out on to Court One in front of a huge crowd, but as soon as the match started, Andy's nerves left him. He played some stellar shots and won the first two sets easily. Radek must have realized he was in danger of losing the match, because he started trying to break Andy's concentration. He played the fool, made silly comments and at one point ran forward to kiss the net!

Court One at Wimbledon

It was no use. Andy won the third set and the match was over. Raděk Štepánek was out of the tournament, and Andy Murray was through to the third round. As if that was not exciting enough, Andy was told that his third-round match would take place on Centre Court, the most famous tennis court in the world.

THE CHAMPIONSHIPS, WIMBLEDON

There are eighteen courts at the All England Lawn Tennis Club in Wimbledon, but Centre Court is the most impressive of them all. It was built in 1881, and is only used for the two weeks of the Wimbledon tournament. The court is surrounded by tiered seating, like you would find at a football stadium. There is a Royal Box for VIP visitors and a players' box for the family and friends of the players. Centre Court also has its own hawk, Rufus, whose job is to chase away pigeons!

Did you know?

• The first Wimbledon tournament was held in 1877.

• The grass on each court is cut to a height of exactly 8 millimetres.

- The men's Wimbledon trophy has a silver pineapple on top.
- During the tournament, over fifty thousand tennis balls are used...
- ...and twenty-three tonnes of strawberries are eaten.

Drama on Centre Court

Andy's third-round opponent on Centre Court was David Nalbandian, a hard-hitting Argentinian player who had once reached the final of Wimbledon. Andy's dad came down from Scotland to watch the match, joining Judy and Jamie in the players' box. Andy knew they were there, but he had no idea who was in the Royal Box – none other than his favourite James Bond actor, Sean Connery!

Jamie Murray

The first set was very exciting. When it reached six games all, there was a tie-break. If a set is drawn six games all, a tie-break is used to decide the winner. Players start at 0–0 and the first person to reach seven points wins the set. If the score reaches 6–6 in the tie-break, play continues until one player manages to surge two points ahead. Andy won the tie-break and the 10,000 people in the crowd went wild.

The second set was even better. Andy was playing his best tennis ever, and he won the set by six games to one. If this had been a junior tournament, two sets would have been enough, and Andy would have won the match there and then. But this was senior Wimbledon, where men play the best of five sets. Andy needed to win one more set.

Andy's problem was, he had never played super-long matches before. He was fast and unbelievably skilful, but he lacked the stamina to keep going for hour after hour. He began to feel tired and cold – and then he got a cramp.

You probably know what a cramp is. You sometimes feel it as a 'stitch' in your side when you have been running for a long time. Footballers occasionally get it in their legs at the end of a long, hard match. Tennis players, too. Andy started to feel intense pain in his muscles, and his legs became so stiff that he could hardly walk, let alone run. The crowd continued to cheer and clap, supporting Andy as best they could, but the match was basically over. David Nalbandian won three sets in a row and the match was his.

Finding Fame

Even though Andy's Wimbledon journey was over, his life had changed for ever. He had been the only British man in the third round of Wimbledon that year, and he had come very close to getting through to the fourth round. The press (TV, news reporters and bloggers) went crazy. The next day, Andy found himself being followed by photographers wanting to get pictures of him.

The James Bond actor Sean Connery phoned Andy and congratulated him on his performance at his first ever Wimbledon. Imagine your screen idol calling you up to say well done!

There was more to Andy's life than tennis, of course. While he was on tour, he met a seventeen-year-old girl called Kimberley Sears, whose dad was a well-known tennis coach. Kim was still at school, studying for her A-levels. She and Andy spent time together whenever they could, and started dating.

ON THE RISE

Back when he was fourteen years old, Andy's ambition was to play at senior Wimbledon. Now that he had done that – and done it well – he needed a bigger ambition. His world ranking had shot up from 317th to 205th. His new goal was to rank among the top 100 players in the world.

In the weeks after Wimbledon, Andy won more and more tennis matches against well-respected players, and his world ranking rose steadily … 164th … 145th … 122nd … 109th … he was already getting close to his target.

That September, Andy travelled to Bangkok, the capital city of Thailand. In Bangkok, Andy beat a player called Robin Soderling, bringing his world ranking to 100. After the match, he sent his mum a simple, four-word text message.

"I DID IT MUM."

When Judy Murray received the text, she was so happy and proud, she burst out crying.

King Fed

As it turned out, Bangkok had more surprises in store for Andy. He got all the way through to the men's singles final, where he played against a twenty-four-year-old tennis ace called Roger Federer. Federer had already won six majors, and he was the undisputed number-one player in the world at the time. Andy had watched 'King Fed' on television many times, but he had never played against him. It felt like a dream.

ROGER FEDERER

Born: 8 August 1981, Basel, Switzerland

Nationality: Swiss

Height: 185 cm

Weight: 85 kg

Plays: right-handed

Highest world ranking: 1

Number of major tournaments: 20

Roger played lots of different sports as a child, including football, badminton and basketball, but it soon became clear that tennis was his real talent. By the age of eighteen he was the best player in Switzerland and by the age of twenty-three he was the best player in the world. He has won Wimbledon more times than any other man, and is known for his elegant play and friendliness. His signature shot is the 'slice backhand', a cunning stroke which keeps the ball low and makes it difficult to return.

It was an entertaining match for the spectators. Andy Murray served seven aces and managed some electrifying passing shots. An ace is when you serve so fast, your opponent cannot even touch the ball with their racket. A passing shot is when your opponent comes towards the net and you hit the ball past them, left or right. A passing shot has to be lightning quick and extremely accurate.

In the end, Roger was simply too good for Andy. He was as strong as an ox, as stealthy as a tiger and as elegant as a ballet dancer. He hit the ball at wicked angles and made it spin in the air so that it bounced off the court in unpredictable ways. On that day in Bangkok, Roger proved once again why he was the world number one.

Andy was not discouraged by his loss to Roger Federer. He had played against the best in the world, and had managed to give him a fright or two. More importantly, getting through to the final had increased Andy's world ranking to seventy-second.

Tiger Tim

Roger Federer was known for being extremely friendly off the court. Another very friendly player was Tim Henman. Tim was an experienced athlete and he had been British tennis number one for a long time. He often gave Andy help and advice, but they had never played each other in a serious match.

That changed at the end of 2005, when Andy and Tim faced each other in the first round of a tournament in Basel, Switzerland. Basel is a sunny city with a beautiful cathedral, but Andy and Tim were not there as tourists. They were there to play.

TIM HENMAN

Born: 6 September 1974, Oxford, England

Nationality: British

Height: 185 cm

Weight: 77 kg

Plays: right-handed

Highest world ranking: 4

Number of major tournaments: 0

As a child, Tim was good at all sports, but he was best at tennis. His family had a grass court in their back garden, so grass was always his favourite surface to play on. From 1998 to 2006, Tim was Britain's number-one male tennis player. His style of play involved the 'chip and charge' tactic, which meant running to the net early in a point to put pressure on his opponent. 'Tiger Tim' reached six major semi-finals, including four at Wimbledon, but never quite managed to get through to a major final. Off the court, Tim was an excellent juggler. He could juggle balls, tennis rackets and even mobile phones.

"THERE ARE NO GREY AREAS WITH COMMITMENT. NINETY-FIVE PER CENT DOESN'T WORK."

Tim Henman, The Telegraph (2014)

Andy won the first set. Tim won the second. The third set went to a tie-break. "Which will triumph?" the commentator asked. "Experience or youth?"

On that day, the answer was youth. Andy played a beautiful drop shot, Tim made a couple of mistakes, and a few minutes later, Andy had won the match.

"Andy Murray is a wonderful player," gushed

tennis commentator Andrew Castle afterwards. "He can win Slams in the future, I think."

In one dream year, Andy had gone from a boy ranked 420th in the world to a man ranked sixty-fourth. He returned to Scotland for Christmas, tired but happy.

ALWAYS LEARNING

Andy Murray is proud of being Scottish. His favourite film is *Braveheart*, a historical epic about a warrior fighting for Scottish independence 700 years ago. In one scene, the warrior William Wallace yells to his men,

"THEY MAY TAKE OUR LIVES, BUT THEY'LL NEVER TAKE OUR FREEDOM!"

Scotland and England have not been at war for centuries but there is still some rivalry between them, especially when it comes to sport. When Scotland play England at football, the atmosphere in the stadium is electric. And when England play Argentina, for example, some Scottish fans wear Argentine football colours.

The rivalry is mostly light-hearted, but on one

occasion it got Andy Murray into trouble. During the 2006 World Cup (for which Scotland had not qualified), a reporter asked Andy who he would be supporting.

"Anyone but England," Andy replied. It was a joke, but some people did not realize that. "Andy Murray is anti-English!" screamed the headlines in the newspapers the following day, and Andy lost a lot of fans. Andy was upset by the reaction to his joke. He had never hated England, and did not want anyone to think he did. He was much more careful in front of television cameras after that experience.

A New Coach

In 2006, Andy got a new coach, a fast-talking American called Brad Gilbert. He was thrilled when Brad said yes to coaching him. For one thing, Andy has always loved America and Americans – he loves their warmth, energy and positive attitude. For another, Brad Gilbert had an excellent track record. He used to coach none other than the blonde-haired, denim-shorted whizz-kid Andre Agassi himself – Andy's hero since the age of seven!

Andy talked with Brad Gilbert about his goals. Now that he was in the top hundred, Andy wanted to go higher still. He was desperate to break into the top ten and to win a Grand Slam tournament. Brad said he would do everything he could to help.

Andy knew that this was no empty promise. Brad had taken Andre Agassi all the way to world number one, with six Grand Slams and an Olympic gold medal.

Brad and Andy talked about what happened in his Wimbledon match against David Nalbandian – the match where he got a cramp in his legs. They both knew that Andy must become stronger and fitter if he was to play long, hard tennis matches against the best players in the world.

Andy was tall, which is good for a tennis player, but he needed to be more muscular. Professional tennis players eat a massive amount of food, which provides them with the energy they need for five-set matches or long workout sessions in the gym. Andy started to eat large amounts of muscle-building food like sushi, protein bars and steak, taking in 6,000 calories every day, spread over six meals! He increased the amount of time he spent in the gym, lifting weights and doing various exercises to become fitter.

Running with 'The Duck'

Andy also worked on his speed. Everyone knows that the ability to run fast is essential for a tennis player. You need to be able to reach the ball in order to have a chance of hitting it, so you must be able to accelerate quickly over short distances.

Luckily, Andy's new coach Brad Gilbert was a friend of the Olympic sprint champion Michael Johnson, one of the greatest sprinters of all time. Michael Johnson had a very upright running style and a short stride. This was the reason for his nickname – 'The Duck'! Michael won almost every race he ever ran, and set world records that lasted for years.

Michael Johnson

Michael agreed to spend a day on a running track with Andy, to help Andy get even faster. He watched Andy run 200 metres and was impressed by what he saw. Andy's running technique was already quite good. Michael gave Andy some extra running tips, and together they devised a training programme that Andy could do on his own. As well as making Andy faster, this training would delay the moment in a match when his legs got tired.

Positive Mental Attitude

Most importantly of all, Brad Gilbert gave Andy advice about attitude. Every tennis player in the top 100 is fast and strong, so the difference between winning and losing often comes down to what is going on in the players' minds. Brad was an expert in this mental side of the game, and had written a whole book about it. He taught Andy about the destructive power of frustration and negativity. If you miss an easy shot, you start to get cross with yourself. You beat yourself up about it. Now there are two players on the court who are trying to take you down – and one of them is you!

Instead, you need to develop what Brad calls 'short-term memory'. If something bad happens, you simply choose to forget it. If you miss a shot, you forget it. If you serve badly, you forget it. You move on, and do better on the next point. Great champions like Serena Williams have learned to do exactly this. If Serena loses a point or a game, she forgets about it and concentrates 100 per cent on winning the next one.

BRAD GILBERT'S BEST ADVICE

1. DRM
This stands for Don't Rush Me. If you rush, you make mistakes, so take your time on the court.

2. "Play like a boa constrictor"
Slowly squeeze the life out of your opponent. Tighten your grip on the match bit by bit.

3. "Don't ask a skinny dog to fly"

Be aware of your weaknesses. If you know your drop shots are poor, don't attempt too many of them.

4. "Beware the wounded bear"

Don't get over-confident too early in the game. Often people play better when they are losing, so watch out!

5. "Kick your own butt"

Tennis singles is a lonely game. You're out there on your own, so take responsibility for motivating yourself. If you don't, no one else will.

Under Brad Gilbert, Andy's ranking went up and up. Before long, he was in the top twenty in the world – and then the top ten. Brad was only Andy's coach for one year, but Andy learned a lot of useful things from him.

Meanwhile, Andy's relationship with Kim was still going strong. Even though Kim was away at university much of the time, she came to watch Andy's matches whenever she could.

A DAY TO REMEMBER

In September 2007, Tim Henman retired from playing tennis after an impressive career. He had made it to number four in the world and had come closer to winning a Grand Slam than any other British man since the 1970s, appearing four times in the semi-finals of Wimbledon.

Naturally, Tim's retirement put the spotlight on Andy Murray as the nation's new best hope of a tennis champion. No British player had won any Grand Slam for seventy-one years, longer than most people could remember.

That champion seventy-one years ago was the great Fred Perry, an Englishman who won Wimbledon not just once but three times running, in 1934, 1935 and 1936. Television was in its early days back then and Wimbledon was not televised, so the only people who saw his victories were the ones who were actually there!

FRED PERRY

Born: 18 May 1909, Stockport, England

Nationality: British, US citizen from 1939

Height: 183 cm

Weight: 78 kg

Plays: right-handed

Highest world ranking: 1

Number of major tournaments: 10

Fred Perry was world table tennis champion at the age of nineteen and then went on to become a tennis champion, winning ten majors. Fred faced prejudice from the English tennis association because he was the son of a cotton spinner and had not attended a posh school. He felt happier in the USA and became an American citizen in 1939. His name endures to this day as a fashionable clothing brand.

"I DIDN'T ASPIRE TO BE A GOOD SPORT; 'CHAMPION' WAS GOOD ENOUGH FOR ME."

Fred Perry (c.1934)

Andy Murray knew about Fred Perry not only from the history books but also because people seemed to talk about Fred wherever Andy went.

"ARE YOU GOING TO DO WHAT FRED PERRY DID, ANDY?"

"SEVENTY-ONE YEARS IS A LONG WAIT, ANDY."

"ISN'T IT TIME FOR ANOTHER BRITISH WINNER, ANDY?"

How on earth could Andy answer these questions, except to say

"I'LL DO MY BEST"?

True Grit

On 30 June 2008, Andy found himself in the fourth round of Wimbledon. He was on Centre Court, facing Richard Gasquet of France, who was ranked tenth in the world. Andy liked playing at Wimbledon because the home crowd always cheered him on. Today, the spectators were in good spirits, hoping to see their hero reach his first ever Grand Slam quarter-final.

Unfortunately for them, the match did not start well for Andy. He lost the first set 7–5 and the second set 6–3. With Andy's opponent serving for the match at five games to four, the crowd had lost all hope.

Not Andy, though. Fighting to keep his chances alive, he started returning Richard's serves more accurately, walloping the ball back and back and back again into his opponent's court. He showed immense grit and managed to break Richard's serve, tying the third set at five games all. Up in the players' box, Andy's girlfriend, Kim, held her breath as the third set went to a tie-break. On the most crucial point of all, Andy played a lob that was slightly too low for comfort. Richard leapt athletically into the air and played a backhand smash, rocketing the ball down into Andy's court.

Against any other player, that smash would have won the point. But remember, Andy Murray had been training with Michael Johnson, one of the fastest men in the world. Like a cheetah chasing down a gazelle, Andy sprinted across the court, way out of camera shot, and managed not just to reach the ball but to blast it past Richard for a winner.

The crowd rose to their feet with screams and whoops of appreciation. Andy raised his hands in the air and roared with triumph and relief. He had won the set. Chants of "Murray! Murray!" echoed around Centre Court. Andy was more pumped up than ever. He was still behind, two sets to one, but he was determined not to go down without a fight. What was it Brad Gilbert used to say? Beware the wounded bear!

TENNIS SCORING

Tennis has a very unusual scoring system. You need four points to win a game, but those points are not counted 1, 2, 3, Game, as you would expect. Instead, you count 15, 30, 40, Game. Stranger still, the starting score is not called 'nil' or 'zero' like in other sports. It is called '**love**'. This probably comes from the French word 'l'oeuf' which means egg (shaped like a zero).

A score of 40–40 is called '**deuce**'. Deuce derives from the French word 'deux' (two) because you now need to go two points clear of your opponent to win. It works like this. After deuce, the next player to score a point gets the '**advantage**'. If the player with the advantage gets the next point, the game is theirs. If the player with the advantage loses the next point, the score goes back to deuce again. A tight game can keep going deuce, advantage, deuce, advantage, deuce, advantage for a very long time indeed.

The wounded bear broke Richard's serve early in the fourth set, and raced through the rest of the set in just over twenty minutes. Somehow Andy had levelled the match at two sets all! The crowd had always been on Andy's side, but this was different. Their support was passionate and thunderous, almost hysterical.

Fifth Set Frenzy

The first game of the fifth set was even more epic than what had gone before. Andy reached deuce on Richard's serve and they played a super-long rally that brought "oohs" and "aahs" from the crowd. Andy played a lob that went so high into the sky it took almost ten seconds to come down. He followed it up with a beautiful forehand pass. Advantage Murray. In response, Richard smacked down a thunderbolt of an ace. Back to deuce.

In theory, a game of tennis can last for ever. It can go deuce, advantage, deuce, advantage until the end of time. In practice, though, there are rarely more than two or three deuces before someone wins the game. On this occasion, Andy played a winning volley on his fifth break point, and the game was his. He clenched his fists and bellowed so hard and loud, it seemed his eyes would pop out.

Clinching a long, hard game gives a player a psychological boost. Andy was firing on all cylinders and the crowd were beside themselves with excitement. Incredibly, almost miraculously, Andy went on to win the fifth set – and the match! Twenty-one-year-old Andy Murray had come back from two sets down against one of the best players in the world, and he was through to his first Grand Slam quarter-final! When the

BBC interviewed him after the match, he could not have been happier.

"RIGHT THERE," HE SAID,
"IS THE BEST MOMENT
I'VE EVER HAD ON A
TENNIS COURT."

Andy Murray, BBC interview (2008)

THE BIG THREE

hen Andy stepped on to Centre Court for his Wimbledon quarter-final two days later, the crowd was hoping for another dazzling performance. But this time Andy faced an even more formidable opponent – the world number two, Rafael Nadal, or 'Rafa' to his friends. Rafael was very muscular. His right arm was strong, but his left arm – the one he used for hitting the ball – was more like a tree trunk than an arm.

RAFAEL NADAL

Born: 3 June 1986, Mallorca, Spain
Nationality: Spanish
Height: 185 cm
Weight: 85 kg

Plays: left-handed
Highest world ranking: 1
Number of major tournaments: 21

Rafael started playing tennis at the age of three, encouraged by an uncle who saw his potential. He won his first major tournament on his nineteenth birthday and has gone on to win twenty-one tournaments over the course of his career – an incredible record.

Thirteen of Rafael's titles were at the French Open, earning him the nickname 'The King of Clay'. He hits powerful forehand shots with heavy spin. One of his most impressive strokes is a 'banana shot' which curves out of the court and back in again!

"I ALWAYS WORK WITH A GOAL – AND THE GOAL IS TO IMPROVE AS A PLAYER AND A PERSON."

Andy had played Rafael three times in other tournaments, and had lost every time, pounded into submission by that extraordinary left arm. To the disappointment of the Centre Court crowd, it happened again this time. Rafael Nadal won the match in three sets and loped off the court. Rafael went on to beat Roger Federer in the final. The match lasted five sets and many tennis fans think it was the highest-quality tennis match in history.

One Step at a Time

Two months after his Wimbledon disappointment, Andy played in the US Open in New York. This time he went one step further, reaching his first Grand Slam semi-final. If Andy won, he would be through to his first Grand Slam final. But his opponent in the semi-final was – you guessed it – Rafael Nadal, the man who had beaten him at Wimbledon. Could Andy beat Rafael in New York?

He certainly could! From the back of the court, Andy struck the ball hard and cleanly, forcing his opponent to make error after error. Andy won the match in four sets and reached his first Grand Slam final. He celebrated with his usual fist pump and a roar of triumph.

In the final, Andy faced Roger Federer, who by now had twelve Grand Slam titles to his name, including the last four US Opens. People jokingly called this match-up 'Murderer' – the first three letters of MURray combined with the last five letters of FeDERER!

The match was played in the famous Arthur Ashe Stadium in New York. With 23,771 seats, this is the largest tennis stadium in the world. From the outset, Federer displayed his usual nimble footwork, combined with an almost murderous aggression. Murray defended as best he could, but it was not his day. "I came up against the best player ever to play the game," he said after losing the match in three sets.

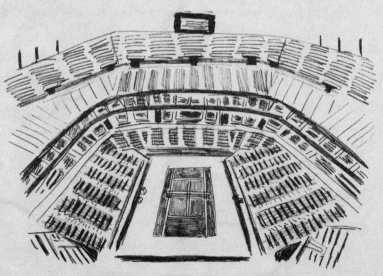

Arthur Ashe Stadium

As always, Federer was generous with his praise.

"I'M SURE WE'RE GOING TO SEE MUCH MORE OF ANDY IN THE FUTURE," HE SAID.

The Serbinator

Andy had made good progress. In one year, he had gone from number eleven in the world to number four. The problem was, the three players above him seemed almost superhuman. Roger Federer and Rafael Nadal had dominated men's tennis for five years already, but now there was a third player to worry about: Andy's friend Novak Djokovic, the Serbinator. This silly nickname mashes together Novak's nationality (Serb) with the name of a killer robot from an old movie (*The Terminator*). It was Novak's on-court aggression and accuracy which led people to make the killer robot comparison.

NOVAK DJOKOVIC

Born: 22 May 1987, Belgrade, Serbia

Nationality: Serbian

Height: 188 cm

Weight: 77 kg

Plays: right-handed

Highest world ranking: 1

Number of major tournaments: 20

Novak Djokovic grew up in war-torn Serbia. He lived with his grandfather and practised his tennis on local courts. His tennis coaches knew he was destined for big things, and they were right. Over the course of his career, Novak has won more prize money than any other player in history: over $150 million. He speaks five languages: Serbian, English, French, German and Italian.

> "I WANT THE SAME THING I'VE WANTED SINCE I WAS SEVEN YEARS OLD. I WANT TO BE NUMBER ONE."
>
> Novak Djokovic (c.2019)

Over the next three years, Andy Murray struggled in the major tournaments, while Novak went from strength to strength. In 2011, Novak won three of the four majors, nearly achieving a

Calendar Grand Slam. One of those titles was the Australian Open, where Novak thrashed Andy in the final.

Tennis writers began to call Federer, Nadal and Djokovic 'The Big Three'. Between them, they were gobbling up almost all of the tournament titles available, leaving very slim pickings for other players. How on earth was Andy ever going to win a Grand Slam title, when he had not one, not two, but THREE such mighty champions to contend with?

TESTING TIMES

The Australian Open in Melbourne is known as the 'Happy Slam' because of its sunshine and its warm, friendly vibes. But in 2011 when Andy Murray was being battered by Novak Djokovic in the final of the Australian Open, he was anything but happy. He swore at the seagulls that circled above the stadium. He shouted at a ball boy. At one point he even yelled "Shut up!" at his mum, who was sitting in the players' box.

Seagulls

Andy was not feeling cross with the seagulls or with his mum. He was feeling cross with himself for not playing as well as he knew he could, and frustrated that his opponent was managing to return some of his best shots. Even though he tried to keep positive thoughts in his head, Andy's frustration kept boiling over – and the TV commentator kept having to apologize for the swear words echoing around the court.

This was not the first time – nor the last – that Andy had yelled and sworn on court. He wrote about his bad temper in his book *Hitting Back*.

"I KNOW IT'S NOT A GOOD EXAMPLE TO SET KIDS," HE WROTE. "I HOPE I CAN STOP DOING IT."

Andy Murray (2008)

TEMPER, TEMPER

Even if a player is frustrated or believes they have been treated unfairly, they have to be careful not to lose their temper. If they shout or swear at the umpire (the person in charge, like a referee in football), they end up having to pay a fine. The size of the fine depends on how bad the behaviour was. Andy Murray has only been fined once in his career, and that fine looks small compared to some.

1987   John McEnroe was fined $17,500 for arguing with the umpire.

2006   Andy Murray was fined $2,500 for swearing at the umpire.

2009   Serena Williams was fined $82,500 for threatening a line judge.

2017   Daniil Medvedev was fined $14,500 for throwing coins at the umpire's chair.

2019   Nick Kyrgios was fined $113,000 for abusing the umpire and smashing rackets.

It was not just Andy who was getting frustrated with his performances. Tennis fans all over the nation were desperate for a British tennis champion. It was now an agonizing seventy-five years since Britain's last men's singles Grand Slam trophy, and it seemed such bad luck that Andy's rise to stardom came exactly at the time when men's tennis was being dominated by the Big Three.

Back home in Britain, some people started being mean to Andy. People called him a loser, not just on Twitter but even in the street. When people call you names like this, the biggest danger is that you start to believe them. "Maybe I am a loser", Andy thought. "Maybe I'll never win a Grand Slam".

It was essential for Andy to surround himself with the right people. He started looking for a new coach, someone who could help him win that elusive major he had dreamed of for so long. Coaches all over the world offered to help him, including a fifty-one-year-old former player called Ivan Lendl.

Coached to Success

∙∙

Andy knew all about Ivan's tennis reputation. Not only had Ivan made it to world number one, he had stayed there for 270 weeks – more than five years. And although Ivan was one of the best players ever to hold a racket, he also understood the pain of losing. Ivan lost four Grand Slam finals before he ever won one. Why did Ivan agree to coach Andy? Firstly, he had met Andy and found him polite and respectful. Secondly, he had no doubt at all that Andy was capable of winning a Grand Slam tournament.

IVAN LENDL

Born: 7 March 1960, Ostrava, Czech Republic

Nationality: Czech

Height: 188 cm

Weight: 79 kg

Plays: right-handed

Highest world ranking: 1

Number of major tournaments: 8

Ivan's parents were top tennis players, and Ivan was their only child. He was one of the most successful tennis players during the 1980s and early 1990s. Nicknamed 'The Terminator', his signature shot was the 'body shot', drilling the ball directly at his opponent's body to win a point. He won many Grand Slam titles, but never Wimbledon.

"IF YOU LOSE, IT HURTS, BUT AS LONG AS YOU FOUGHT HARD, YOU CAN STILL FEEL GOOD ABOUT YOURSELF."

Ivan Lendl (c.2018)

With Ivan coaching him, Andy played sensational tennis. He won the Brisbane International tournament, dedicating his win to "Mr Lendl". He also reached the final of the Dubai Tennis Championships and the final of the Miami Open.

But as you know, it was the four majors which Andy cared about the most. Imagine his excitement in July 2012 when he reached the Wimbledon final, becoming the first male British finalist there since Bunny Austin in 1938. Could he go one step further and lift the trophy? Andy was convinced the answer was yes.

WIMBLEDON 2012

If Andy was to win the Wimbledon final – and the whole tournament – he would have to beat the greatest grass player of all time, Roger Federer himself. 'King Fed' had already won Wimbledon an incredible six times: 2003, 2004, 2005, 2006, 2007 and 2009. If Federer won the tournament a seventh time, it would be a record.

Dozens of celebrities turned up to watch this historic match. Kate, the Duchess of Cambridge, sat in the Royal Box with her sister Pippa. Prime Minister David Cameron and the Mayor of London Boris Johnson were there, and so was the most famous footballer-popstar couple in the world, David and Victoria Beckham. In the players' box sat Andy's mum, Judy, his dad, William, his girlfriend, Kim, Ivan Lendl and the rest of Andy's team. Roger Federer had some supporters, too – his parents, his wife, Mirka, and his coach, Paul.

Centre Court was packed, as was 'Henman Hill'. Named after Tim Henman, this grassy bank in front of a giant television screen was where those without tickets had gathered to watch the match. At exactly 2 pm they broke into a deafening cheer as Andy Murray and Roger Federer walked out on to the court. The match started brilliantly for Andy. He broke Roger's serve in the very first game, and again in the ninth. Ivan Lendl used to be known for his 'body shots' – whacking the ball straight at his opponent – and Andy seemed to have learned this trick from his new coach. He blasted one shot straight at Roger's head from close range – thankfully Roger was able to duck before the ball knocked his head off.

When Andy won the first set, the crowd rose to their feet in delight. For the first time in his life, Andy Murray had won a set in a Grand Slam final. The only person not smiling was Ivan Lendl. Famous for his calmness and composure, Ivan sat there motionless, his chin resting on his hand. It was too early to get excited.

The second set was extremely close,

culminating in a twenty-shot rally in the twelfth game. Roger won the point with a cunning drop shot and took the set seven games to five. With the score evenly balanced at one set all, the spectators on Henman Hill began to put up their umbrellas. The famous British rain had arrived.

In the old days, rain used to cause long interruptions to Wimbledon finals, but then a clever, sliding roof was built over Centre Court. Now the tournament officials can open the roof when the weather is dry and close the roof when it starts to rain.

In the 2012 Wimbledon final, the closing of the roof probably gave Roger a slight advantage. It became like an indoor tennis match, with not a breath of wind, and that suited Roger's style of play. To the dismay of the spectators on Centre Court and Henman Hill, Roger played a set and a half of nearly perfect tennis. He won the third set 6–3 and the fourth 6–4. King Fed had won a record-breaking seventh Wimbledon title. He collapsed on the grass in disbelief, then jumped up to embrace Andy at the net.

Tears on Centre Court

BBC tennis reporter Sue Barker came on to the court to interview the players. The runner-up always goes first, so Andy bravely took the microphone and began to speak. "I'm going to try this," he said, his voice already cracking with emotion, "and it's not going to be easy. I'm getting closer…"

Imagine seeing your dream crushed and then having to make a speech about it. Andy was trying to smile through his tears, but another wave of emotion hit him. He choked up and could not get another word out. Up in the players' box, Kim clapped her hand over her mouth, blinking back her own tears.

The crowd saw that their hero was struggling, and they interrupted with a massive round of applause. They wanted Andy to know that they loved and supported him, Wimbledon champion or not. The bedraggled spectators on Henman Hill joined in as well, jumping up and down and waving their arms. The clapping and cheering went on for thirty incredible seconds, giving

Andy a chance to dry his tears. When he lifted the microphone to his mouth again, he praised his magnificent opponent, Roger Federer. "He's not bad for a thirty-year-old," he joked, then added in a more serious tone, "Congratulations, you deserve it."

Andy also thanked those in the players' box: his mum, his girlfriend, his coach and the rest of his team. "I'm going to try and not look at them," he said, "because I'll start crying again!" His next comments were for the crowd who had supported him all afternoon. "Last of all, to you guys…" he said, his voice still trembling.

"EVERYBODY ALWAYS TALKS ABOUT THE PRESSURE OF PLAYING AT WIMBLEDON, AND HOW TOUGH IT IS, BUT IT'S NOT THE PEOPLE WATCHING WHO MAKE IT TOUGH … THEY

MAKE IT SO MUCH EASIER TO PLAY. THE SUPPORT HAS BEEN INCREDIBLE, SO THANK YOU."

OLYMPIC HERO

The Wimbledon final had bruised Andy physically as well as emotionally. He took a week off after the tournament, to let his body and mind recover. He could not rest for long, though. London was hosting the Olympic Games in 2012 and Wimbledon was getting ready to welcome tennis players from all over the world. The dark green fences around the tennis courts were replaced by bright purple ones, bearing the Olympic logo.

The five rings of the Olympic logo represent the five areas of the world that participate in the games: Europe, Africa, Asia, the Americas and Oceania.

The opening ceremony of the Olympics was a dazzling spectacle, a celebration of all things British, including James Bond, the Queen and Mr Bean. Athletes usually attend the ceremony in person, but Andy chose to stay away. At the Beijing Olympics in 2008 he had made the mistake of tiring himself out at the opening ceremony and losing his first tennis match. He did not want to do the same again.

Team GB (short for Great Britain and Northern Ireland) did well at the London Olympics, winning more medals than ever before. Andy did amazingly, too, reaching not one but two finals: men's singles and mixed doubles.

MIXED DOUBLES

In mixed doubles, a man and a woman play as partners against another pair. Mixed doubles was first created in the nineteenth century as a safe way for young men and women to meet and get to know each other. Now it is a popular and competitive form of tennis, fun to play and fun to watch. The man and the woman have to work together as a team, and their skills complement each other. In professional tennis, there are no world rankings for mixed doubles, but there is still some prize money on offer.

The night before playing in the men's singles final, Andy watched the track and field athletics in the Olympic Stadium. In forty-four magical minutes, Team GB won three gold medals: Jessica Ennis won the heptathlon (an event made up of seven different tests of speed and strength), Mo Farah stormed to victory in the men's 10,000 metres, and Greg Rutherford won the men's long jump. Team GB was smashing it!

The next morning, everyone woke up smiling. Super Saturday had been amazing, and now Great Britain had the chance of another gold medal, this time in tennis. Who was Andy's opponent in the fight for an Olympic gold medal? Roger Federer, of course! It was four weeks to the day since Roger had beaten Andy on this very court and been crowned Wimbledon champion. But today felt different, for three important reasons:

1. Roger Federer had never won an Olympic gold medal before, so he and Andy were in the same situation for once.

2. Roger's semi-final had been exhausting. It had lasted four and a half hours, the longest match in Olympic history.

3. Andy's tears after the Wimbledon final had won the hearts of the nation. They loved him like 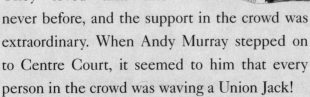 never before, and the support in the crowd was extraordinary. When Andy Murray stepped on to Centre Court, it seemed to him that every person in the crowd was waving a Union Jack!

The sun was shining. The roof was open. Music blared from the speakers around the court. Wearing the blue shirt of Team GB with a Union Jack on one sleeve, Andy looked relaxed and focused. He looked like a man who had a job to do and knew exactly how to do it. The match started. Andy played confident, flowing tennis, and won the first set, just as he had done at Wimbledon. But this time, instead of letting Roger back into the match, Andy became even more aggressive in his play. Lobs, smashes and cross-court passing shots flowed from Andy's racket. Incredibly, a whole hour passed without Roger winning a single game.

Roger Federer once said that when you play against Andy Murray, no two points are the same. This unpredictability was making Andy difficult to beat. Andy won the second set and surged ahead in the third. Before he knew it, he was ahead by two sets to love and five games to four. Just one more game and the Olympic medal could be his.

Slam, Bang, Wallop!

If Andy felt nervous stepping up to serve for gold, he did not look it. He won the first point, 15–0, then Roger won a point to even the score. 15–15. Andy readied himself to serve, tossed the ball into the air, swung his racket and—

SLAM!

The ball whizzed down the middle of the court at a hundred and thirty miles per hour. Roger lunged towards it, but in vain. The ball ricocheted off the frame of the racket and flew up into the cheering crowd. 30–15 Murray.

Andy wiped his face with a towel, chose a ball and readied himself to serve again. He tossed the ball into the air, swung his racket and—

BANG!

The ball zoomed out wide this time, landing in the corner of the service box and hitting the purple fencing before Roger even had a chance to swing his racket. Ace! The crowd went wild. 40–15 Murray.

It was match point. Andy wiped his face, chose another ball and readied himself to serve. He tossed the ball into the air, swung his racket and—

WALLOP!

Another zinger down the centre of the court, so fast it was basically a blur. Roger leaped to his left and stuck out his racket, but the ball was already gone. Ace!

Game, set and match, Andy Murray!

ACES

An ace in tennis is a valid serve that the receiver cannot even touch with their racket. It usually happens when a player serves lightning fast and manages to place the ball in one of the far corners of the service box. Of course, if you serve an ace, you win the point immediately. Like an ace in card games, it is unbeatable.

American giant John Isner holds most of the records when it comes to aces. John is over 2 metres tall and jumps off the ground when he serves. When you whack the ball from that high up, the ball can bounce on the other side of the net and fly right over your opponent's head!

In women's tennis, Serena Williams has the best serve in history. In her 2012 Wimbledon semi-final victory, she served an impressive twenty-four aces.

Andy had succeeded in doing something that Roger Federer had never managed. He had won an Olympic gold medal. Andy's Olympics was not over yet. He had the mixed doubles final that same evening, playing alongside the hard-hitting eighteen-year-old Laura Robson.

LAURA ROBSON

Born: 21 January 1994, Melbourne, Australia

Nationality: Australian and British (dual nationality)

Height: 180 cm

Weight: 67 kg

Plays: left-handed

Highest world ranking: 27

Number of major tournaments: 0

When Laura moved to the UK at the age of six, she was already a keen tennis player. In 2008, she won junior Wimbledon, on the same day that Rafael Nadal and Roger Federer played their famous final. Laura was known for her determination and her powerful hitting of the ball. She had her best years as a tennis player in 2012 and 2013. Unfortunately, she has struggled with injuries since then.

"IF I DON'T PLAY WELL, THEN IT'S NOT THE END OF THE WORLD ... THERE'S ALWAYS NEXT WEEK."

Laura Robson, press conference (2015)

During the London Olympics, Andy and Laura had already won three entertaining mixed doubles matches. They narrowly lost the final but still came away with silver medals. "It's been an incredible week for both of us," said Laura after the match. "We're proud to represent Great Britain."

Queen Elizabeth Olympic Park

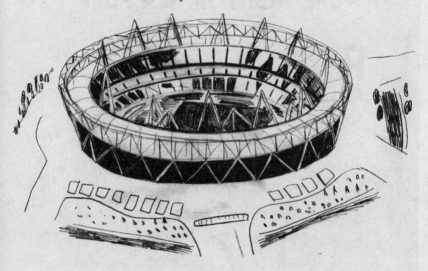

ONE NIGHT IN NEW YORK

At the Olympics, Andy had beaten Roger Federer on Roger's favourite surface, grass. He had done it coolly and calmly, in front of 500 million television viewers worldwide. That's half a billion people! No surprise, then, that Andy was feeling good when he travelled to New York later that month for the US Open. Ever since winning the junior US Open as a boy, he had loved playing in America.

As Andy progressed through the tournament, he managed to beat some of the best players in the world – Milos Raonic, Marin Čilić and Tomáš Berdych. The Berdych match was extraordinary because the wind was so strong. Hot dog wrappers, paper cups and plastic packaging were flying through the air. A chair blew on to the court. Two ball boys holding an umbrella were nearly swept off their feet.

It was hilarious but also frustrating. The ball

kept slowing down in mid-air and veering off in weird directions. More than once, Tomáš tossed the ball into the air to serve and then missed it completely. Andy managed to deal with these bizarre conditions better than his opponent, and ended up winning the match in four sets. Sir Sean Connery interrupted Andy's interview after the match to congratulate him. Sir Alex Ferguson – the most well-known football manager in the world at that time – was with him. The reporters were gobsmacked to see three of the most famous Scotsmen of all time chatting together like old friends.

Andy was through to his first men's US Open final, where he would have to face his old friend Novak Djokovic. While Roger Federer was still the toughest opponent on a grass court, and Rafael Nadal on a clay court, Novak was by far the best hard-court player in the world. He was the reigning US Open champion and the reigning Australian Open champion. He had won twenty-seven matches in a row at hard-court Grand Slams, and had every intention of making it twenty-eight.

Andy's childhood hero Andre Agassi wished

him well before the match. "If there's anyone who deserves a Slam, it's Andy ... I'd love to see him get over the finish line."

The Arthur Ashe Stadium after dark is one of the most glorious sights in the tennis world – a dazzling bowl of light. It is noisy, too, especially with over 23,000 raucous fans cheering their heads off. On the night of the Murray-Djokovic final, those fans included Andy's old friend Sir Sean Connery and his new friend Sir Alex Ferguson. The much-anticipated final lived up to everyone's expectations. Andy won the first and second sets. Novak won the third and fourth. As Andy struggled in the fourth set, he looked up at the players' box and yelled at the top of his voice, "My legs feel like jelly!" So many people tweeted about that moment, #Jelly started trending worldwide!

A fifth set would decide who lifted the trophy. Would it be Andy's first Grand Slam victory, or would it be Novak's fifth?

I'm Not Going to Lose This!

Andy decided to walk off court for a quick

toilet break. He stood at the sink and looked in the mirror. "I'm not going to lose this!" he said to his reflection. It was a moment of pure determination. Andy was making a solemn promise to himself that he would go back out on to that court and give everything he had to win the title. He was going to serve with every ounce of strength in his arms. He was going to run until he dropped. He was going to use every scrap of skill and cunning he possessed – and leave the court with no regrets.

Andy came out of that toilet a new man. He sensed that Novak was getting tired, so he focused on making him run from side to side as much as possible, just as his American hero Andre Agassi used to do to his opponents. Left, right, left, right: Andy kept smacking the ball back into Novak's court.

His perseverance paid off. Andy managed to break Novak's serve three times in the deciding set, and built up a significant lead: five games to two. The two men had been playing for nearly five hours, and Novak's right leg was beginning to cramp. A trainer arrived to give the painful leg a massage. As for Andy, he was already back on the court, bouncing up and down, eager to get on with the match. The crowd were also on their feet, clapping and hopping in the cold night air. What an amazing atmosphere!

Ever since he was a young boy watching Andre Agassi on TV, Andy had imagined how it might feel to serve for a major championship. Now that the moment was finally here, he felt strangely relaxed. As weary Novak took his place at the other end of the court, Andy prepared to serve. The game started like a dream. Andy won the first point with a backhand smash, and the second point with an ace. On the third point, Novak over-hit one of his shots and the ball went out.

40–0. Three championship points. Three chances to make history under the floodlights in New York. The first of the three crucial points was won by Novak with a ferocious forehand smash. Cramp or no cramp, the Serbinator was not going down without a fight.

40–15. Still two chances for Andy to make history. Andy tossed the ball into the air and served straight at his opponent. Novak slammed it back a little too hard, and the ball landed just outside the white lines of the court.

It was all over. Game, set and match, Andy Murray.

Andy crouched down, motionless, his face in his hands. He had done it. On the fifth time of trying, Andrew 'Young Warrior' Murray had won a Grand Slam final. He was the 2012 US Open champion. In the changing room after the match, Andy celebrated with his team. There were hugs and kisses all round, and lots of laughter. Even the iron-faced Ivan Lendl was smiling. "I'm so proud of you," Ivan told Andy. "You played a great match and showed real fighting spirit."

That night, Andy went to a Chinese restaurant with Kim, his family and his whole team. His victory had earned him nearly two million dollars in prize money, but for Andy it was never about the money. He was just happy to have achieved his goal of winning a Grand Slam. As he tucked into his crispy duck salad that night, Andy realized that all of the sacrifices he had made – all of those painful training sessions and exhausting international flights – had been worth it.

Return to Dunblane

On the first Sunday after winning the US Open, Andy Murray returned to his childhood home, Dunblane. People came out in their thousands to meet him. They stood in pouring rain, waiting for him to arrive. At long last, an open-top bus came into view. On top of the bus was the man they had been waiting for. He was wearing a baggy sweatshirt, a pair of dark blue jeans – and two Olympic medals. Andy Murray got off the bus in the town centre and posed for photos beside the gold-painted post box, which had been installed in honour of his Olympic success. He shook hands with hundreds of people, high-fived dozens of children and signed what seemed like a thousand autographs.

Most of those in the crowd remembered Andy as a small boy, hanging around in his gran's toyshop on the high street or playing tennis on the artificial grass at the sports club but they all wanted to celebrate Andy's big win at the US Open.

THE A TEAM

The success of any sportsperson is a result of thousands of hours of training and practice. The world saw Andy Murray performing heroically on the tennis court, but they never saw the activities that made this heroism possible – hours and hours of painful, sweaty training, day after day after day.

Andy knew how important training was, and he assembled a team of people who would make him as good as he could possibly be. Alongside his tennis coach, he needed a skilled physiotherapist, a trustworthy hitting partner and a ruthless physical trainer.

Physiotherapist: A physiotherapist (or 'physio') is someone who treats injuries using massage, exercise, heat and cold. Andy's physio for many years was another Andy, Andy Ireland. They spent at least an hour and a half together every day, making sure the tennis star's body was in tip-top condition.

Hitting partner: One of Andy's best friends at school in Spain was Daniel 'Dani' Vallverdú. After they left school, Dani became a trusted member of Andy's team. When Ivan did his coaching sessions with Andy, Dani was the one on the other side of the net, responsible for hitting the ball back to Andy over and over again! Dani also helped Andy to research his opponents and devise tactical plans for how to beat them.

Trainer: Top tennis players are so closely matched that even a tiny improvement in strength or speed could end up being the difference between winning or losing a match – or a tournament. Andy understood this, and he was 100 per cent committed to his training regime. Andy's trainer Jez Green was responsible for overseeing all of Andy's work in the gym.

Strength

Jez devised gruelling exercise routines to make

Andy stronger. For example, he made Andy do chin-ups with a 20-kilogram weight strapped around his waist. Most people cannot do even one chin-up, but Andy can do twenty-seven in a row. His chest and shoulders grew much more muscular as a result of all these chin-ups.

Speed

A tennis match is not one long run. Instead, it consists of hundreds of little sprints, one after another. Jez realized that Andy was exceptionally fast over short distances. A tennis court measures just over 8 metres from one side to the other, and Andy can cover this distance as fast as any man in the world – even professional sprinters!

Stamina

In 2012, Andy bought a full-body exercise machine called a Versaclimber. Using this machine is like climbing a never-ending ladder, and it wears you out like nothing else on earth.

Flexibility

Andy did 'hot yoga' sessions in a sauna heated to

40 degrees Celsius. He followed a list of twenty-six body positions, including some very tricky poses like the 'rabbit' and the 'toe stand'. Trying to hold these positions in the intense heat made him feel like he was going to faint.

Whenever Andy moaned about these nightmarish workouts, Jez replied, "You'll be thanking me before long." Jez knew that every tennis trophy Andy lifted was a result of his perseverance in the gym. As it happened, there was still one particular tennis trophy that Andy wanted to lift more than any other: the Gentlemen's Singles Trophy at Wimbledon.

Wimbledon
Gentlemen's
singles
Trophy

WIMBLEDON 2013

Let's face it, for many British tennis fans, Wimbledon is the only tournament that really counts. We get wildly excited about tennis while Wimbledon is on TV, but as soon as the trophies have been awarded, we switch off and forget about tennis for the next fifty weeks!

Even though Andy Murray had become the first British man in seventy-six years to win a Grand Slam tournament, the questions about Wimbledon did not show any signs of stopping. "Is now your best chance of winning Wimbledon, Andy?" "Could you be the first British champion for seventy-seven years, Andy?" "Is 2013 your year, Andy?"

No wonder Andy felt stressed and nervous as the grass court season began. He managed to win the Queen's Club Championships, which is seen as a warm-up tournament for Wimbledon, but of course that only piled on more pressure.

It was a relief for everyone when the

Wimbledon tournament finally started. Andy got through the first round comfortably, beating Benjamin Becker of Germany in three sets. And while Andy was playing that match on Centre Court, something incredible was happening on Court One next door – Rafael Nadal was beaten in three sets by an almost unknown Belgian player called Steve Darcis. Rafael was out of the tournament!

In the second round, it was Andy's turn to be on Court One, where he managed to win against Lu Yen-hsun of Taiwan. Next door on Centre Court, another huge upset was taking place: Roger Federer, the greatest grass player of all time, was beaten by Sergiy Stakhovsky (who had played Andy all those years ago in the final of the junior US Open). It was probably the greatest shock in the history of Grand Slam tennis, not least to Sergiy himself. After the match, he declared with a smile, "I can tell my grandkids that I kicked the butt of Roger Federer!"

Andy beat Tommy Robredo (Spain) in the third round and Mikhail Youzhny (Russia) in the fourth. His quarter-final was against another

Spaniard, the left-handed Fernando Verdasco. Andy lost the first two sets but managed to come from behind and win three sets in a row. Sir Alex Ferguson, the manager of Manchester United, watched the match from the royal box, and was very impressed by Andy's comeback.

Andy's semi-final opponent was Jerzy Janowicz from Poland. Jerzy was over 2 metres tall and was the fourth fastest server of all time – his very first serve of the match was a 139 mile per hour ace. Andy was not afraid, though. One of his greatest strengths had always been the ability to return humongous serves. Andy won the match three sets to one, and reached his second Wimbledon final.

Two of the Big Three (Rafael Nadal and Roger Federer) were out of the tournament, but Novak Djokovic was still in it. For the first time ever, Andy and Novak were about to do battle for the men's singles Wimbledon title.

Let's Make History

The day of the final was beautifully sunny, not at all like the grey skies of the previous year's event. The seats around Centre Court filled up with excited tennis fans, and Henman Hill was so full of people, barely any grass was visible. No one was calling it Henman Hill, though. Its new name, at least for that day, was 'Murray Mound'. Some people had queued for over nine hours to guarantee themselves some space on that famous grassy slope.

Footballers, politicians and Olympic athletes were taking their places in the royal box, and just when it seemed like there was no more room for celebs, two Hollywood film stars rocked up. One was the Scottish actor Gerard Butler, star of films like *How to Train Your Dragon* and *300*. The other was Bradley Cooper, star of *Guardians of the Galaxy* and *Avengers: Infinity War*. Bradley is a huge tennis fan and attends Grand Slam matches whenever he has the opportunity. The two film stars sat next to each other, chatting and laughing. Gerard told Bradley that he was a friend of Novak Djokovic but that today he would be supporting Andy. As a proud Scot, how could he do otherwise?

Most of the other spectators around the court

were supporting Andy, too. Union Jacks were everywhere – fluttering on sticks, poking out of straw hats and even painted on people's cheeks. The message on one girl's T-shirt spelled out the thought on everyone's mind:

"LET'S MAKE HISTORY!"

Andy and Novak were waiting at the players' entrance to Centre Court. Not for the first time, Andy gazed at the inscription carved above the door, a quotation from an old poem:

IF YOU CAN MEET WITH TRIUMPH
AND DISASTER

AND TREAT THOSE TWO IMPOSTERS
JUST THE SAME

Treat triumph and disaster just the same? Andy reflected grimly. That's easier said than done!

The clock struck two and the players walked out on to the court to rapturous applause. There were shrieks of "I love you, Andy!" and one shout of "You're a genius, Andy, a genius!"

The umpire Mohamed Lahyani was already sitting in his lofty seat at the side of the court. He gave the players five minutes to warm up, then started the match. Mohamed Lahyani was already famous, having umpired the longest match in the history of tennis. In the first round of the men's singles at Wimbledon 2010, John Isner and Nicolas Mahut battled for eleven hours and five minutes before Isner won. As Andy and Novak took their rackets from their kit bags and started their warm-up routine, they must surely have been hoping they could win the match in less than eleven hours!

THE FINAL

Andy and Novak were closely matched at the start. Both of them were hitting the ball right from the back of the court, producing long, tiring rallies. It was hot on court, and at times Andy felt as if he could not breathe. One thing gave him hope, though. Novak seemed to be making a few errors. It was only a point here and a point there, but it was enough for Andy to win the first set by six games to four. Up in the Royal Box, Gerard Butler and Bradley Cooper applauded enthusiastically and took a selfie together to mark the moment.

The second set was harder. The Serbinator broke Andy's serve and surged ahead to a 4–1 lead. But the iron-willed Scot was not giving up. He fought back one point at a time, delighting the crowd with a series of impossible-looking passing shots. As yet another forehand winner thudded against the canvas at the back of the court, Judy Murray punched the air and bellowed encouragement at her son.

Andy won the second set 7–5 and the crowd broke into a raucous, sing-song chant: "Let's go, Andy! Let's go, Andy! Let's go, Andy! Let's go, Andy!"

The third set was so tense, it was almost unbearable. Both players broke serve twice, bringing them level at four games all. In the game that followed, Andy continued to battle, chasing every ball with utter determination. Not only was he reaching these balls against all odds, he was executing his shots with accuracy and skill. A delicate drop shot here, a vicious volley there, Andy kept choosing the right shots at the right moments.

"THE CROWD WAS RIGHT IN MY HEAD NOW. I COULD SENSE THEIR SUPPORT, THEIR DESIRE, THEIR DRIVE. I WANTED TO GET THEM OVER THE LINE."

Andy Murray, *My Road to Wimbledon Glory* (2013)

Up in the royal box, Gerard Butler and Bradley Cooper were on their feet. They applauded aces and winced at errors. They goggled at break points and gaped at cross-court passing shots. When Andy broke Novak's serve to bring the score to 5–4, the TV cameras captured their almost comical reaction. Gerard's jaw dropped open and his eyebrows shot up in total astonishment. Bradley gaped left and right as if to reassure himself that this was not a dream.

One Game More

It was not a dream. Andy Murray was one game away from winning Wimbledon.

The beginning of the next game seemed too good to be true. Andy went 15–0 up, then 30–0. To the delight and disbelief of the crowd, a colossal serve down the middle of the court stretched that lead to 40–0. Andy had three championship points – three chances to end the agony of Britain's seventy-seven-year wait for a men's singles champion at Wimbledon.

The first championship point was a thrilling

rally. Novak came to the net and somehow managed to guess three times which way Andy was going to hit the ball, before playing a winning volley of his own.

40–15. Two more championship points. On the next point, Andy missed his first serve and Novak hit a backhand winner off the second.

40–30. One more championship point. The next rally could have gone either way. Andy went for a winner – a backhand passing shot down the line – and missed it by a few centimetres.

Deuce.

"I WILL REMEMBER THOSE FIRST THREE MATCH POINTS FOR THE REST OF MY LIFE. HE LOST THEM ALL. I COULD HEAR MY HEART THUMPING."

Judy Murray, *Knowing the Score* (2017)

As Andy towelled his face and prepared for

his next serve, he realized that his left hand was trembling violently. He had missed three golden opportunities to win Wimbledon, and nervous energy was coursing through his muscles.

"You're OK!" shouted his mum.

But Andy was not OK. Novak Djokovic no longer had anything to lose and he was playing superbly. In the points that followed, Novak returned serve accurately, struck the ball with startling ferocity and played winners at angles that looked quite impossible. He even had some help from the net, when a hopeful half-volley flicked off the cord and dropped down on Andy's side.

Like that ball teetering on the top of the net, deciding which way to fall, this whole match hung in the balance. Advantage Djokovic. Deuce. Advantage Djokovic. Deuce. Advantage Djokovic. Deuce. Andy had the impression that if he lost this game, his chance of winning Wimbledon would have gone as well. The crowd did their best to lift his spirits. "Mur-ray! Mur-ray! Mur-ray!" they chanted.

On the next rally, Novak slammed the ball

fiercely into the far corner of Andy's court, then the other corner. Defending for his life, Andy flicked a lob high into the air, but Novak was right underneath it, preparing to smash it back. Andy stayed in the backhand corner, hoping the ball would come his way – and it did. The young warrior from Dunblane belted a two-handed cross-court backhand and followed it up with a stinging forehand. Advantage Murray.

It was championship point yet again. Union Jacks and Saltires waved. The crowd were on their feet, applauding Andy's resilience. "Come on, Andy!"

Andy towelled himself down and took several deep breaths. When he was ready, he tossed the ball into the air and slammed a massive serve right into the corner of the service box. Against almost any other player, it would have been an ace, but the Serbinator flung out his racket and managed to return the ball. Andy played a less-than-perfect forehand and Novak prepared to hit a backhand winner straight down the line. Except, it did not go down the line. It went into the net.

Game, set and match, Andy Murray.

Sweet Victory

Andy dropped his racket, flicked off his cap and lifted two clenched fists in triumph. Joy and relief flooded his exhausted body. He had done it. Novak walked around the net and gave the champion a congratulatory hug. He knew how much this first Wimbledon victory meant to Andy. In a strange sort of way, he was pleased for him.

As the crowd continued to applaud and cheer, Andy squeezed past the scoreboard, high-fived a row of ecstatic fans, muscled up on to the roof of the commentary box and headed towards his friends and family. He needed to share this moment with the people who loved him most, those who had stuck with him through good times and bad.

Andy hugged Ivan, Kim and everyone in his team – or so he thought. As he made his way back down towards the court, people started shouting, "Andy, your mum! Don't forget your mum!" It was an innocent mistake, but one that Judy Murray would tease him about for the rest of his life. His mum was the one who had first put a tennis racket in Andy's hand, the one who had driven him and his friends to tournaments in a minibus emblazoned with Saltires, the one who taught him the magnificent two-handed backhand he had used on that last crucial deuce. The hug, when it finally came, was a long and very emotional one.

FAMILY MAN

As Andy Murray lifted the Wimbledon trophy that summer afternoon, Twitter exploded with happy, congratulatory messages.

Stephen Fry, actor and writer: "Glory glory glory glory glory GLORY be!!! Andy Murray, you beauty!"

Miranda Hart, comedian: "I KNEW he would do it. Still reeling. Thanks, Andy Murray, for making my/our summer. Wowzers!"

Sadiq Khan, later mayor of London: "Congratulations to my one-time doubles partner Andy Murray on his glorious Wimbledon victory!"

Jade Thirlwall, singer: "Massive congrats to Andy Murray and his team! Brilliant game. Proud moment for Britain."

Jimmy Carr, comedian: "Andy Murray has just made me cry. The man is a god. I'm so happy."

The newspaper reports the following morning contained the same mixture of delight and disbelief. Every front page had a picture of Andy and the trophy. "After 77 years, the wait is over!" declared The Telegraph, while the main headline in The Guardian consisted of just one word: CHAMPION.

Newspapers reporting Andy's 2013 Wimbledon win

Winning Wimbledon catapulted Andy to superstardom. He was invited to the Wimbledon Ball (a fancy dinner for the champions and their families), to chat shows and comedy shows, fashion shoots and charity appearances, and even to 10 Downing Street (the Prime Minister's house). This was not the first time that Andy had visited 10 Downing Street. He had gone there in 2010 and played tennis in the dining

room with Prime Minister David Cameron. The Prime Minister hit the ball really hard and Andy was terrified of breaking the glass chandeliers that hung from the ceiling!

Andy's best Christmas present of 2013 was the BBC Sports Personality of the Year award, which is given each year to a British sportsperson who has achieved something amazing. Accepting the

BBC Sport Personality award

award, he made fun of his famously monotonous voice.

> "NO MATTER HOW EXCITED I TRY TO SOUND, MY VOICE STILL SOUNDS INCREDIBLY BORING ... I'M VERY HAPPY AND EXCITED RIGHT NOW."

A New Approach

Not for the first time, Andy decided it was time for a new coach. This time, he asked the French tennis ace Amélie Mauresmo to coach him. At first, Amélie thought he was joking. For one thing, she had never coached before. For another, no top male tennis player had ever appointed a female coach.

For Andy, having a female coach was no big deal. His mum had coached him when he was a boy, and he had always thought it strange that there were not more female coaches in tennis. Besides, he was not offering her the job because she was a woman. He was offering her the job because she was calm, intelligent and brilliant at tennis.

AMÉLIE MAURESMO

Born: 5 July 1979, Paris, France

Nationality: French

Height: 175 cm

Weight: 69 kg

Plays: right-handed

Highest world ranking: 1

Number of major tournaments won: 2

Amélie was a great tennis player with a strong serve and a fearsome backhand. She used to get called a 'choker' – a player whose nerves cause them to lose from winning positions – but in 2006 she overcame those nerves to win the ladies' singles title at Wimbledon. In 2021, she was appointed director of the French Open, the first female director of any Grand Slam tournament.

Unfortunately, when the new tennis season began, Andy did not play as well as he knew he could. For the first time in six years, he failed to reach the Wimbledon semi-final, and later that year he dropped out of the top ten in the world rankings. Some people said that Andy's poor results were Amélie's fault. This infuriated Andy. He announced that his bad results were his fault alone, adding that people never used to blame his male coaches for slumps in form.

STICKING UP FOR WOMEN

The world of professional tennis used to be very unfair. The prize money available to female tennis players was tiny compared to what male players were getting. Now it is much more equal, but not completely. Andy is a feminist – someone who believes that men and women should always be treated equally.

- He has fought for female tennis players to get the same prize money as male players.

- He thinks there should be more women's games on Centre Court at Wimbledon.

- He corrects people when they forget about women's tennis. When a reporter congratulated him for being "the only person to win two Olympic tennis gold medals", Andy pointed out that Venus and Serena Williams had won four each!

Wedding Bells

. . . .

Of all the strong women in Andy Murray's life, the most important was still Kimberley Sears. Most people knew Kim as the glamorous girl in the players' box at Andy's matches. The TV cameras at Wimbledon loved zooming in on her bright blue eyes and shiny golden hair. Fashion bloggers wrote millions of words about her chic clothes and handbags.

Obviously, there was more to Kimberley than her looks and accessories. For one thing, she was a talented painter, who specialized in painting animals on enormous canvases. "I appreciate art of every kind," she said, "but I love to create paintings myself that are bold, upbeat and meaningful – and often very large."

On 11 April 2015, Kim and Andy got married in Dunblane Cathedral. They held their wedding reception at Cromlix House, a five-star hotel just outside Dunblane. Andy had bought the hotel two years earlier, to create jobs for local people and to give his friends and family somewhere nice to stay whenever they visited Dunblane.

Cromlix House

Davis Cup Victory

Getting married did wonders for Andy's tennis. In 2015 he played several matches for Great Britain in the Davis Cup and helped the British team get all the way through to the final series of matches against Belgium. Andy won a thrilling doubles match with his brother Jamie, and went on to beat Belgian legend David Goffin in the final singles match.

People had warned Andy that the roof in the arena was too low to play lobs, but that did not stop him. After a long rally on match point, he flicked an inch-perfect lob right over David Goffin's head. As the ball bounced just the right side of the baseline, Andy fell to the floor and was mobbed by his ecstatic teammates. Unfortunately, Andy's worst fear is being pinned down, unable to move his arms and legs, so when his Davis Cup teammates piled on top of him like footballers

The Davis Cup

144

celebrating a winning goal, Andy's face appeared completely panic-stricken!

Becoming a Father

On 7 February 2016, Andy's life changed for ever. His wife Kim gave birth to their first child, a daughter. They named her Sophia. Andy was thrilled to be a father, and he loved spending time with little Sophia. But his constant globetrotting meant that he saw much less of her than he wanted. Of all the sacrifices he had made as a professional tennis player, this was by far the hardest.

It is well known that Novak Djokovic and Roger Federer played better tennis after they became fathers. Perhaps becoming a father gives sportspeople a better perspective on life. They realize that tennis is not the most important thing in the world, so they are able to go out and play without pressure.

So it proved for Andy, too. While baby Sophia played at home, Andy played some of the best tennis of his life. In July that year, he got all the way through to the Wimbledon final, where he played the tall Canadian Milos Raonic. Milos was feeling full of confidence after his semi-final, having beaten none other than Roger Federer with a barrage of rocket-like serves and cunning volleys. But Andy had played against powerful servers before, and he knew he had a good chance of victory.

When the match began, Milos was frustrated to see even his fastest serves being blasted right back to him. In the middle of the second set, he smashed down a ferocious bazooka of a serve which the radar gun measured at 147 miles per hour, the second fastest serve in Wimbledon history (the fastest ever was 148 miles per hour). Incredibly, Andy managed to return the ball – and win the point!

Andy playing at Wimbledon

An hour and twenty minutes later, Andy and Milos walked forward and embraced each other at the net. Andy had won the match in straight sets, 6–4, 7–6, 7–6, earning himself his second Wimbledon title!

Back in 2013, Andy had lifted the golden trophy on behalf of a desperate, victory-starved nation. Now, in 2016, he was lifting it for himself and for his family and friends. As he looked up at his loved ones in the players' box, Andy savoured every moment. "Nothing tops becoming a parent for the first time," he said afterwards, "but Wimbledon's a close second!"

The following month, Andy flew to Rio de Janeiro in Brazil, in search of a second Olympic gold medal. He got through to the final, where he faced Argentinian giant Juan Martín del Potro. It was a gruelling match, which his mum Judy described as "four hours of torture". Once again, Andy emerged victorious, becoming the first man to win two back-to-back tennis golds at the Olympic Games.

If further proof were needed that fatherhood was good for his tennis, Andy ended his season by winning all of his last five tournaments and achieving the world ranking he had always dreamed of. To the delight of his fans, Andy Barron Murray had reached the absolute pinnacle of men's tennis. He was number one in the world.

INJURIES AND SETBACKS

Playing professional tennis puts a lot of stress on your muscles and joints, and Andy Murray has experienced more than his fair share of injuries. After winning Wimbledon for the first time, he had terrible pains in his lower back, and had to undergo surgery to make it better.

After winning Wimbledon for the second time, his hip became the problem. Dodgy hips are common among tennis players, because of all the twisting and sprinting they do. As the pain worsened, Andy stopped enjoying tennis and was eventually unable to play at all. In June 2017, he hobbled out of Wimbledon and was told by a doctor that he would never play professional sport again.

In the months that followed, Andy struggled even with simple things like putting on his socks and shoes. Playing with his children was hard, and playing tennis was out of the question. He underwent surgery on his hip, but the pain did not get better. At the Australian Open in 2019, Andy gave a tearful press conference, where he spoke about the pain and expressed doubts about his future.

"Might this be your last tournament?" one of the reporters asked.

"There's a chance of that, for sure," Andy replied. The thought of ending his tennis career in this way was almost as distressing as the physical pain. Shortly after the Australian Open, Andy had surgery again. This time the surgeon inserted a metal plate into his hip. The second operation was more successful than the first. For the first time in years, Andy found that he could move around freely and without pain.

After an operation like that, the process of rebuilding strength is long and slow. As Andy exercised in his private gym at home, he kept thinking about the doctor who had told him he would never play professional sport again. He was determined to prove that doctor wrong.

The Comeback King

It was almost six months before Andy was ready to play again. In June 2019, he tested his fitness by entering the men's doubles tournament at Queen's. Andy's doubles partner was a brilliant Spanish player called Feliciano Lopez. British tennis fans were happy when Andy and Feliciano won their first match, and overjoyed when they went on to win the tournament. Andy Murray was back!

At Wimbledon two weeks later, Andy entered the mixed doubles, this time with the legendary Grand Slam champion Serena Williams. "She's the best player ever," he said, "so she'll be a pretty solid partner!" Serena liked Andy too, not just because of his tennis achievements but because of all the times he had spoken up for women's rights.

SERENA WILLIAMS

Born: 26 September 1981, Saginaw, USA

Nationality: American

Height: 175 cm

Weight: 72 kg

Plays: right-handed

Highest world ranking: 1

Number of major tournaments won: 23

Serena and her older sister Venus Williams came from a poor family in Compton, Los Angeles, USA. Their father, Richard, taught them tennis at a young age and both sisters became amazing players. At the end of 2002 Serena was ranked number one in the world and Venus was number two. Serena has lifted trophies in four different decades, and her fans know her simply as 'the Queen'.

"VICTORY IS VERY, VERY SWEET. IT TASTES BETTER THAN ANY DESSERT YOU'VE EVER HAD."

Serena Williams (c.2017)

People called this exciting new partnership MURENA (the first three letters of MUR-ray and the last three letters of Ser-ENA). Murena won their first two Wimbledon matches, playing some of the fiercest and most entertaining tennis ever seen on a mixed doubles court.

At one point, the tall Frenchman Fabrice Martin served a 138 miles per hour bullet into the far corner of the service court, and Serena belted it right back for a cross-court winner. Most people would not even be able to see a ball moving that fast, let alone return it – one of the many reasons why Serena's fans call her the Queen. It seemed likely that Andy and Serena would go on to win the tournament, but they were eventually beaten by the tournament favourites, Bruno Soares and Nicole Melichar.

COVID-19 Pandemic

At the start of 2020, the world was turned upside down by a deadly new virus called COVID-19. The tennis season was suspended and Andy returned to his family home in Oxshott, Surrey. Andy had a gym and a tennis court at home, so he was able to keep in shape during lockdown. But instead of facing Djokovic,

Federer or Nadal across the net, he now found himself playing against Kim and their children!

At the height of lockdown, Andy and Kim created a video challenge for the nation, which they called the hundred volley challenge. You have to stand opposite a partner and hit a tennis ball between you one hundred times without the ball touching the ground. Thousands of people around the world attempted the challenge, including Novak Djokovic and his wife, Jelena!

Andy and Kimberley Murray

LOOKING BACK

At the start of 2022, Andy Murray's ranking is outside the top 100. Will he be able to fight his way back into the top 100? What about the top ten? Given Andy's age and his recent injuries, you might imagine that a return to the top ten would be impossible. Be careful, though. Andy is one of the most determined sportsmen ever, and he has done seemingly impossible things before. Remember that match against Richard Gasquet, when he came back from two sets to love and five games to four down? Beware the wounded bear!

Besides, Andy's injuries have changed his perspective on the game. The reason he plays tennis these days is not to win tournaments, nor even to achieve a high world ranking. The reason he plays is because he loves tennis. If Andy can stay healthy, he can continue to train. If he can continue to train, he can continue to play matches. And if he can continue to play matches, he will continue to feel happy and fulfilled.

Whilst continuing to do his best in tennis tournaments, Andy enjoys spending time with his family. He and Kim now have four children: Sophia (born in February 2016), Edie (born in November 2017), Teddy (born in October 2019) and a third daughter whose name is still a secret (born in March 2021).

The Big Four?

In this book you have met three of the most amazing tennis players ever to swing a racket. At the time of writing, Rafael Nadal has won twenty-one Grand Slam tournaments and Roger Federer and Novak Djokovic are level at twenty wins each. Any of them may go on to win more Grand Slams.

Andy Murray on the other hand has won just three Grand Slams: the US Open in 2012 and Wimbledon in 2013 and 2016. But here is the thing you need to remember: Andy Murray won those tournaments at a time when the Big Three were completely dominating men's tennis. On a good day, he could go toe to toe with any one of them, and be victorious.

When professional tennis players talk about 'The Big Four', they are including Andy Murray in that group. Every time Andy stepped on to a court with Roger, Rafael or Novak, the whole world knew that Andy was capable of beating them.

Would Andy have won more tournaments if the Big Three were not standing in his way? Of course he would. But any sportsperson wants to compete against the best of the best, and Andy had the privilege of competing against not one but three of them.

Andy's Legacy

'Legacy' is a word for a person's impact on the world, and how they will be remembered. When Andy Murray eventually retires from professional tennis, we know how he will be remembered. And yes, it has to do with Fred Perry!

- When Andy won the US Open in 2012, he became the first British winner of a Grand Slam men's singles title for seventy-six years, since Fred Perry in 1936.

- When he won Wimbledon the following year, he became the first British winner of a Wimbledon men's singles title for seventy-seven years, since Fred Perry in 1936.

Add to that two back-to-back Olympic gold medals, and Andy's legacy is nothing short of magnificent. No wonder he won the BBC Sports Personality of the Year Award a record-breaking three times. Andy's success has inspired a whole new generation of British tennis players:

Cameron Norrie

When Cameron first turned pro, Andy Murray came up to him in the changing room to say hello, and offered to practise with him.

Liam Broady

When Liam qualified for the Miami Open, Andy texted him immediately to say well done. Andy had been live-streaming Liam's match on his computer!

Kyle Edmund

Andy allowed Kyle to use his Miami base for winter training, and made himself available to answer Kyle's questions.

Jack Draper and Emma Raducanu

Andy Murray joined with Amazon Prime Video to offer a 'Future Talent Award' for up-and-coming players. Jack and Emma received 60,000 pounds in funding from this award. "Andy is such an inspirational person to look up to," said Emma.

Andy does everything he can to support younger players, but he never offers advice when it is not needed. When a reporter asked Andy if he had any advice for Emma Raducanu, he gave a simple, one-word answer: "No."

EMMA RADUCANU

Born: 13 November 2002, Toronto, Canada

Nationality: British

Height: 175 cm

Weight: 55 kg

Plays: right-handed

Highest world ranking: 18

Number of major tournaments won: 1

Emma moved to the UK at the age of two, with her Chinese mother and her Romanian father. As a child she enjoyed basketball, go-karting, skiing, horseriding, ballet and tennis. At the age of just eighteen, she stunned the tennis world by winning the US Open without losing a single set. Emma is an aggressive player, who likes to stand on the baseline and hit the ball hard and flat. Her signature shot is her backhand down the line.

> "I DON'T FEEL ANY
> PRESSURE ... I'M JUST HAVING
> A FREE SWING AT ANYTHING
> THAT COMES MY WAY."
> Emma Raducanu (2021)

Charity Work

Andy has done lots of charity work, particularly for Malaria No More, which fights to end malaria. Malaria is a disease spread by mosquitoes, and kills around 800 children every day, mostly in Africa.

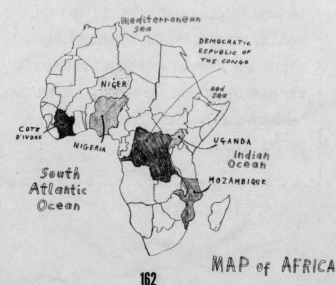

MAP of AFRICA

When Andy became a father, he decided he would do everything he could to raise money for mosquito nets that would stop children in Africa being bitten by infected mosquitoes. Andy says:

"I HOPE THAT IN YEARS TO COME WE CAN LOOK BACK AND KNOW THAT WE WERE THE GENERATION THAT HELPED TO END DEATHS FROM MALARIA."

Andy Murray (c.2016)

Andy also sometimes plays charity matches to raise money for good causes. One time, in the middle of a charity doubles match against his coach Ivan Lendl, Andy gave Ivan a taste of his own medicine, with a deliberate body shot! "Oof!" grunted Ivan as Andy's lightning bolt hit him on the chest. Andy was thrilled. He ran around the court, punching the air and whooping with delight. Then he turned to Ivan and chirped, "Sorry!" In 2019, Andy received a knighthood for his services to tennis and charity. A knighthood (or damehood for women) is an honour given by the Queen to someone who has served their country in an outstanding way. Andy's full name is now 'Sir Andrew Murray', but he does not insist on the 'Sir' part!

Racket or Wand?

When all is said and done, perhaps the most significant part of Andy's legacy is one that is impossible to measure – the happiness he has given to those who have watched him play. After one exquisite Murray drop shot (played in Madrid against Tomáš Berdych), an American TV commentator gasped, "Is that a racket in Andy's hand or is it a magic wand?"

If you have ever seen Andy play tennis – on TV, on YouTube or even in person – you have probably asked yourself the same question.

TIMELINE OF ANDY MURRAY'S LIFE

15 May 1987 Birth

December 1999 Wins the Orange Bowl tournament

September 2002 Goes to train in Spain

September 2004 Wins the junior US Open

June 2005 Wins two matches at his first Wimbledon

September 2005 Breaks into the top 100 in the world

February 2006 Becomes British number one

April 2007 Breaks into the top ten in the world

June 2008 Reaches first major quarter-final (Wimbledon)

September 2008 Reaches first major final (US Open)

January 2012 Hires Ivan Lendl as coach

July 2012 Loses to Roger Federer in Wimbledon final

August 2012 Beats Roger Federer to win Olympic gold

September 2012 Beats Novak Djokovic to win first major title (US Open)

July 2013 Beats Novak Djokovic to win first Wimbledon title

June 2014 Hires Amélie Mauresmo as coach

April 2015 Marries Kim Sears

November 2015 Leads Great Britain to Davis Cup victory

February 2016 Sophia Murray is born

July 2016 Beats Milos Raonic to win second Wimbledon title

September 2016 Beats Juan del Potro to win Olympic gold

November 2016 Becomes world number one

June 2017 Doctor tells him he will never play pro tennis again

November 2017 Edie Murray is born

January 2018 Undergoes first hip surgery

January 2019 Undergoes second hip surgery

June 2019 Wins men's doubles title at Queen's with Feliciano Lopez

July 2019 Partners Serena Williams in Wimbledon mixed doubles

October 2019 Teddy Murray is born

March 2020 COVID-19 lockdown begins

March 2021 A fourth Murray child is born

ANDY MURRAY'S END-OF-YEAR WORLD RANKINGS

Year	Ranking
2003	540
2004	411
2005	64
2006	17
2007	11
2008	4
2009	4
2010	4
2011	4
2012	3
2013	4
2014	6
2015	2
2016	1
2017	16
2018	240
2019	125
2020	122
2021	134

If

"IF YOU CAN MEET WITH TRIUMPH
AND DISASTER

AND TREAT THOSE TWO IMPOSTERS
JUST THE SAME"

The inscription above the players' entrance to
Centre Court at Wimbledon is a quotation from
one of the nation's favourite poems, 'If' by Rudyard
Kipling. Here is the poem in full.

If you can keep your head when all about you
Are losing theirs and blaming it on you;
If you can trust yourself when all men doubt you,
But make allowance for their doubting too;
If you can wait and not be tired by waiting,
Or being lied about, don't deal in lies,
Or being hated, don't give way to hating,
And yet don't look too good, nor talk too wise:

If you can dream, and not make dreams your master;
If you can think, and not make thoughts your aim;
If you can meet with Triumph and Disaster
And treat those two imposters just the same;

If you can bear to hear the truth you've spoken
Twisted by knaves to make a trap for fools,
Or watch the things you gave your life to, broken,
And stoop and build them up with worn-out tools;

If you can make one heap of all your winnings
And risk it on one turn of pitch-and-toss,
And lose, and start again at your beginnings
And never breathe a word about your loss;
If you can force your heart and nerve and sinew
To serve your turn long after they are gone,
And so hold on when there is nothing in you
Except the Will which says to them: "Hold on!"

If you can talk with crowds and keep your virtue,
Or walk with kings, nor lose the common touch,
If neither foes nor loving friends can hurt you,
If all men count with you, but none too much;
If you can fill the unforgiving minute
With sixty seconds' worth of distance run,
Yours is the Earth and everything that's in it,
And, which is more, you'll be a Man, my son!

Rudyard Kipling

GLOSSARY

Ace: a serve that is not touched by the opponent.

Advantage: a player gets the 'advantage' in a game when they win a point after the game has gone into deuce.

Air raid: an attack during wartime, in which bombs are dropped from an aircraft onto the ground.

Break of serve: when a player wins a game in which their opponent was serving.

COVID-19: one of a family of viruses – coronavirus – that sometimes moves from animal to humans. COVID-19 is a new virus that affects humans.

Deuce: this term comes from the French word deux, which means two. In tennis deuce, refers to a tied match where both players have 40 points, and the game is at 'deuce'. To win the game a player needs two more points, one point to get the advantage and another point to win the game.

Double fault: if a player's second serve lands outside of the service box or doesn't clear the net it's known as double fault and they lose the point.

Drop shot: a softly hit shot where the tennis ball lands just over the net.

Fault: when a player serves, if the ball lands outside of the service box or doesn't clear the net it's a fault. If this happens on a player's first serve they can take a second serve.

Feminist: someone who believes and tries to affect change to ensure both genders receive equal opportunities and treatment.

Grand slam: this term refers to the four most important annual tennis events. They include the Australian Open, French Open, US Open and Wimbledon. The term 'Grand Slam' also refers to the accomplishment of a tennis player winning one of these championships. If a player wins all four of these championships within a calendar year this is known as a 'Calendar Grand Slam'.

Lob: a shot that goes over your opponent's head.

Love: a tennis term used instead of the word 'zero'. Both players begin a game with zero points, which is known as 'love'.

Malaria: a disease passed to humans through a mosquito bite, malaria causes illness and sometimes death.

Match point: a point which if won by a tennis player will also win them the match.

Passing shot: a shot that goes past your opponent on either side.

Press conference: a meeting between an athlete and the media, where the media asks the athlete questions.

Prime minister: democratically elected head of a government.

Professional: (in sporting terms) an athlete who receives payment for their performance in sporting events.

Queen: the female ruler of a country.

Rally: a series of back and forth shots between players once a point has begun, a rally will continue until a point has been won.

Ranking: a system for measuring the performance of the best players in the world.

Serve: a shot that will start a tennis game. Players alternate serving each game.

Tennis academy: a kind of school that focuses on tennis, some academies also provide educational facilities.

Virus: a simple life form that can invade the body, where they multiply and cause disease.

War: an armed conflict between different countries.

INDEX

ABOUT THE AUTHOR

Stephen Davies worked in West Africa for thirteen years and now lives in London with his wife and daughters. His books include *Survivor: Titanic* and *The Ancient Egypt Sleepover*.

During Stephen's childhood, the TV was always on during the two weeks of the Wimbledon tournament. He remembers warm summer afternoons watching tennis with his mum, cheering on Andre Agassi and Steffi Graf.

Stephen loves playing chess and reading detective stories. He often visits schools to encourage young people in their own creative writing.